TEENAGE ALCOHOLISM AND DRUG ABUSE

CAUSES, CURES AND CONSEQUENCES

A handbook for parents of teenagers that explores the reasons that teens become involved with drugs and alcohol and how to prevent it. It helps identify some of the warning signs and offers advice on where to go for help.

BY JOHN BARTIMOLE

Frederick Fell Publishers, Inc.
2131 Hollywood Boulevard
Suite 204
Hollywood, Florida 33020

PUBLISHER
Frederick Fell Publishers, Inc.
Donald Lessne
Chairman/Publisher

EDITOR
Susan Snider

COPY EDITORS
Debbie Bohl
Kathryn Leth

TYPESETTING
Thomas Gordon Associates, Inc.
Miami, Florida

ADVERTISING DIRECTOR
Barbara Newman

DESIGNER
Kathy Funes

ADVERTISING AGENCY
Frederick Fell Advertising

All rights reserved. No part of this work covered by the copyright herein may be reproduced or used in any form or by any means—graphic, electronic, or mechanical, including photocopying, recording, taping or information storage and retrieval systems—without permission of the publisher.

Distributed by Kable News Company, 777 Third Avenue, New York, NY 10017

TABLE OF CONTENTS

Preface xiii

Introduction 1

Chapter One 3
Teenage Alcoholism and Substance Abuse:
An Overview

Chapter Two 13
The Language of Drugs

Chapter Three 27
The Short- and Long-Term Effects of Drugs

Chapter Four 45
Alcohol and its Effects

Chapter Five 51
The Warning Signs of Substance Abuse

Chapter Six 65
Why Kids do Drugs and Alcohol

Chapter Seven 75
If You Suspect Your Child Is Abusing Drugs

Chapter Eight 85
What Parents Can Do To Help Prevent Alcohol
and Substance Abuse

Chapter Nine 99
What Schools Must Do To Help

Chapter Ten 111
Where Do We Go From Here?

Table I – Depressants 115

Table II – Hallucinogens 116

Table III – Inhalants 117

Table IV – Cannabis 118

Table V – Stimulants 119

Table VI – Narcotics 120

Resources 121
Publications, Individuals

Resources 123
Organizations

INTRODUCTION

"My interest is in the future, because I'm going to spend the rest of my life there."

Charles F. Kettering, the legendary automotive giant, couldn't have been more precise in describing our feelings about the future, either. The future is always full of optimism, of hope, of better days.

We agree, too, with Disraeli, who once wrote, "Youth is the trustee of posterity."

Put those two quotes together, and you have our inspiration for writing this book: youth, and the future.

Both are integrally tied together. And both are threatened by alcohol and drug abuse.

Current statistics show us that about one of every three teenagers in the country is involved in some kind of substance abuse, be it alcohol or any other drug. That's a frightening statistic, because such abuse tears at the very potential of youth.

We all know what drugs can do. We've seen Len Bias cut down in the prime of his life, a victim of cocaine. All of us know someone whose life has been wasted by alcohol, too. We've seen the human misery caused by substance abuse, the broken dreams, the shattered promises, the potential wasted.

This book is our effort to help parents educate their children against the dangers of drug abuse. You see, we have a great deal of faith in children. First of all, they're smarter than we often give them credit. Consequently, it's our belief that, given the proper information, most children will not abuse drugs or alcohol.

In our first book on the subject of problems facing parents, "Preventing Missing Children," one of the chapters was entitled "Education: The Best Form of Prevention." Though we don't use that particular title anywhere in this book, it certainly would be appropriate.

And so, education is what this book is about. We believe this work will be of significant help in helping parents to educate their children about the dangers of drug abuse.

By doing that, we are helping to safeguard our youth, our trustee of posterity.

And we also help guarantee the future of our youth, ourselves and our country.

After all, that's where all of us will spend the rest of our lives.

—Carmella R. Bartimole
—John E. Bartimole

June 10, 1987

CHAPTER ONE

TEENAGE ALCOHOL AND SUBSTANCE ABUSE: AN OVERVIEW

"Just say no." Three words, packed with a ton of life-saving advice. That message is probably the single most important one we can share with our children as we help them in their battle against drugs and alcohol.

Believe this is a battle, because it is a titanic struggle for our children to resist the instant-high lure of drugs and alcohol. In our "pill for every ill" society, children are conditioned to believe that pain can be overcome by the ingestion of a tablet, a drink, or a drug. The old-time wisdom that some pain—be it emotional or physical—is a necessary and natural part of growth is virtually nowhere to be found.

And so, we now tell our children to "just say no," and that is a message we must repeat and repeat, *ad infinitum*, to this, and subsequent generations of children.

But we must go beyond the simple, powerful phrase. We must, as parents, caregivers and those who love children, understand addiction and the consequences of drugs and alcohol, of these enemies which threaten to undermine the stability and vitality of our youth. We must grasp the whys and hows of abuse, and put ourselves in the place of our children to empathize with—and combat—the pressures they face when they attempt to "just say no."

GOING BEYOND THE FACTS

Mere knowledge of the fact that drugs can kill obviously isn't enough to dissuade some people from using them. The death of Len Bias, the University of Maryland basketball star, to cocaine should have had a profound impact on his peer group—other outstanding athletes. But almost within a wink of Bias' death, Don Rogers, the talented safety of the Cleveland Browns, also died, a victim of cocaine. Since then, still others have died or admitted to cocaine abuse.

Scandals in the National Basketball Association (NBA), which has the most stringent drug-enforcement policy of any professional sports league, also prove that the fear of detection or loss of livelihood isn't always adequate to preclude or end drug abuse.

Instead, it must be a combination of several ingredients—education, understanding, legal penalties—and, importantly, a child's own self-esteem—which must form the recipe to help our youngsters resist drugs and alcohol.

Certainly, no one could argue that the substance abuse problem can be wrested under control with a three-word phrase, no matter how wise and sound it is. What's needed, then, is an understanding of the myriad facts about abuse: how drugs work; what their appeal is to our children; what their short- and long-term effects are; what the tell-tale signs of abuse are; how to handle your child if you suspect (s)he's abusing drugs; what type of help to seek for drug abusers; and—perhaps most importantly—what we can do to prevent abuse before it begins.

And we must delve deeper than that. We must appreciate the vital role that poor self-esteem plays in the abuse puzzle, and take steps to make sure that we do not denigrate our children's personal sense of worth. We must learn the importance of communication between parents and children, and how to open those vital channels and help prevent substance abuse.

This book examines those, and other, issues. But before anyone can purport to learn about abuse and how it ensnares and affects our children, it's necessary to take a sobering—and somewhat frightening—look at the havoc drugs and alcohol wreak on our children.

A LOOK AT THE STATISTICS

Each year, 10,000 young people between the ages of 16 and 24 are killed in alcohol-related accidents, making it the leading cause of death for this age group. Think about that statistic for a moment. Ten thousand young people claimed by alcohol. And that figure doesn't include "accidental" deaths—such as drownings, suicides, fires, etc.—in which alcohol is implicated. Also not included are the 40,000 young people who are injured annually in alcohol-related traffic accidents. Our society prides itself—and rightfully so—on fervently battling with its collective might the scourges of our children. We donate time and money generously to organizations attempting to find cures for leukemia, other cancers, muscular dystrophy, and all the reprehensible diseases which snuff out the lives of our precious children.

Yet, the leading cause of death of the 16–24 age group—those young people who are just blossoming into adulthood—is now only beginning to be addressed on a national, and urgent, basis.

TEENS AND ALCOHOL

While the most tragic consequence of abuse, death is certainly not the only devastation imposed by alcohol and drugs. The actual number of high schoolers using alcohol is also eye-opening, and may portend future problems.

Studies show that nearly 20 percent—or about 3.3 million adolescents ages 14–17—have serious alcohol problems. Fifteen percent of 10th–12th graders, about 1.6 million students, ingest five or more drinks at least once a week. Three of every four high school students use alcohol, and 93% of all children will at least try alcohol once before graduation.

One of the most authoritative studies on the use by high school students of alcohol was conducted by the Research Triangle Institute (RTI) in 1978; subsequent studies have demonstrated that the results of the RTI group remain valid today.

Among the findings of the survey:
—by 10th grade, most students have at least tried alcohol;
—consumption of alcohol increases signficantly between 10th–12th grade, predominantly among high school boys between 10th and 11th grade;
—the Northeast and North Central states appear to have the heaviest alcohol abuse among high schoolers;

—high school students in the suburbs are more likely to use alcohol than their big-city counterparts;

—drinking has been traditionally viewed as primarily a male problem. While more high school boys drink than their female counterparts, the gap is shrinking as more females turn to drinking.

UNDERSTANDING THE IMPLICATIONS

Why should we be concerned about alcohol and youth? After all, isn't its ingestion encouraged on TV? Don't many people use it as a relaxant? Isn't it almost socially unacceptable to refuse a drink?

Of course, we should be concerned about alcohol consumption, particularly among our youth. What must be remembered—but what is often forgotten or ignored—is the fact that alcohol is a drug, as much of a drug as cocaine or marijuana. The difference is that alcohol is legal, and the majority of other "recreational" drugs are not.

Another cause for concern is that the youth drinkers of today may become the problem drinkers and alcoholics of tomorrow. Most experts agree that there are about 10 million alcoholics in this country, with a similar number of problem drinkers. The costs imposed by these 20 million Americans are staggering, and probably incalculable. Loss of productivity, missed work days due to hangovers, and long-term health problems associated with alcohol abuse, such as cirrhosis of the liver, are just a few of the factors that enter into the fiscal equation when determining the cost of alcohol abuse to society.

More chilling—and extracted at a much higher price—is the loss of lives each year to the ravages of alcohol abuse, either through death caused by a physical ailment or by an alcohol-related accident.

Can we combat alcoholism? Didn't this country once try to live without alcohol, and found it couldn't? Is there such a thing as responsible drinking?

The answer to all three questions is yes. Unfortunately, drinking is too much a part of our societal web to be totally eliminated from our way of life. But we, as parents and as caregivers, can enormously affect the way our children view alcohol.

THE ROLE OF THE PARENT AS A MODEL

In fact, one of the best methods to help young children avoid abusing alcohol is proper parental example. Children, as the adage wisely reminds us, live what they learn: if alcohol is treated by their parents for what it is—a drug which, if abused, can become dangerous and perhaps fatal—children will learn the healthy respect which must be given alcohol. And they'll be better prepared to "just say no" to alcohol and other drugs. We'll examine the entire issue of parental influence on children's use and attitudes toward alcohol and other drugs in Chapter 8.

While alcohol abuse is, in sheer numbers, the most serious drug problem facing our youth, the misuse of illegal drugs, such as marijuana, cocaine, heroin and crack, carries with it the threat of much more immediate—and dire—consequences.

Most of us have heard about the cocaine-induced deaths of Len Bias and Don Rogers; we have listened to experts warn children (and us) that even the first-time use of as powerful a drug as cocaine can kill. Yet, the abuse of illegal drugs continues.

DRUGS AND TEENAGERS

Specific statistics for use of illegal drugs among high school youths are somewhat fuzzy. That may be somewhat attributable to the very illegality of the drugs, which may prevent high school students from admitting their use, even through confidential questionnaires.

But some statistics are evident. The 1978 RTI survey, for example, tells us that half of all high school seniors used marijuana at least once, and that there appears to be a correlation between heavier drinking and the use of marijuana.

The National Institute on Drug Abuse reports that between 1978–82, almost 16 percent of 13-year-olds used marijuana. By the time they're seniors, 61 percent of the students have used drugs.

In 1985, the Institute for Social Research found that nearly 17 percent of high school seniors had used cocaine. And the use was on a marked upswing, after dipping slightly in 1984.

What does it all add up to? More than two of every five—actually, 41 percent—of 1985 high school seniors reported using drugs in the last year, while 26 percent indicated use in the last month.

And the statistics for the general population—which includes youth—are just as telling. For example, Americans now consume more than half (60 percent) of the world's illegal drugs. Twenty million Americans regularly use marijuana, about six million abuse cocaine, and approximately 500,000 are in the clutches of heroin. Three out of every 10 college students will try cocaine at least once, while about three of every four Americans will try an illegal drug by the age of 25.

The introduction of new—and even more potent—drugs, including crack and designer drugs, only exacerbates the problem and compound its consequences. Experts say, for example, that about one million Americans have tried crack, which produces a cheap, intense, and addictive high.

The statistics, then, form a good news/bad news scenario: the good news, say researchers, is that the overall use of narcotics has not risen since 1980. The bad news, though, is quite bad: the drugs are cheaper and more powerful now, which translates into steeper addiction—and fatality—rates.

As a result, the young people of our country have embraced drugs with a fervor unmatched throughout the rest of the world. The National Institute on Drug Abuse describes the relationship between drugs and our youth quite succinctly and dramatically:

"Clearly, this nation's high-school students and other young adults still show a level of involvement with illicit drugs greater than can be found in any other industrialized nation in the world."

The abuse of any drug—be it legal or illegal, alcohol or cocaine—by our youth is particularly intolerable, because it can quickly lead to long-term problems. While adults, for example, may take up to 10 years to become addicted to drugs or become an alcoholic, teenagers may get to that critical point in less than a year.

Again, the losses caused by abuse of drugs are incalculable, but undoubtedly staggering. The money, the time, the lives wasted by drug abuse can never be reclaimed, but we must try our best to prevent such fiscal and physical carnage in the future.

This book is not a panacea, nor does it claim to be. What it does, however, is analyze and explain between two covers, the many interwoven factors which contribute to abuse among our youth. It arms you, the parent or caregiver of a child, with the knowledge, information and methods necessary to help your child to "just say no" to drugs.

We will study, in our next chapter, the definitions of the many terms we have all heard bandied about in conversations about drugs. Precise definitions are important to the understanding of each drug, and to our battle against drug abuse.

CHAPTER TWO

THE LANGUAGE OF DRUGS

The drug culture has a language uniquely its own. Just more than a generation or so ago, being "stoned" meant you were drunk. Now, it usually alludes to being "high" on marijuana or some other psychoactive drug.

Understanding the language of drugs is of critical importance in the overall parental battle against abuse, for several reasons. First of all, in order to understand drugs, their effects and why they're addictive, it's necessary to understand the terms used in conjunction with the substances. Secondly, the use of slang drug terms by teenagers, while certainly not a positive indicator of drug use, should serve as a warning signal to parents. Also, the ability to understand and use the slang expressions when talking to your children puts them more at ease, and further opens the all-important lines of communication.

A GLOSSARY OF DRUG TERMS

Here are some of the terms you should be familiar with:

Drug: a drug is a chemical which produces a change in a person's thoughts or emotions. It can be in virtually any form—pills, liquids, powder—but the substance, in order to be classified as a drug, cannot be a food. Sugar, for example, has been proven to have physiological and psychological effects on people, but is not considered a drug because it has nutritive value and is therefore classified as a food. Conversely, alcohol is a drug—not a food— because it has no nutritive value whatsoever.

Dependence: Physical or psychological dependence on a drug may result when the person has used that drug for a period of time, which varies according to the abused substance.

Certain drugs, including opiates and barbituates, prompt a physical dependency, which means that the drugs actually become a part of the body chemistry. Once the drug is withdrawn, a physically-dependent person will become ill; this stage of physiological trauma is recognized as withdrawal.

When a certain drug becomes the focal point of the abuser's existence, then psychological dependence has occurred. A psychologically-dependent person will become bored, restless, depressed or nervous.

Addiction: occurs when the abuser is psychologically and/or physically dependent on a drug.

Withdrawal: The process an abuser goes through when eliminating the drug of dependence from his life.

Tolerance: Over a period of time, the body learns to tolerate the presence of a particular chemical, thereby forcing the person to use increasing amounts of the drug to achieve the desired "high" or effect. Or, the abuser may combine drugs, with chilling consequences. Those who have developed a high tolerance for cocaine, for example, often resort to taking other drugs to counteract the unpleasant effects of the increased dosage of cocaine.

Side Effects: refers to the other-than-desired results caused by a drug. For example, the effect desired by a user of marijuana is a feeling of euphoria; a side effect (among dozens associated with the drug) is the possibility of flashbacks weeks, and even months, later.

Pusher: one who sells drugs. Amazingly, a recent study reported that 57 percent of high school students bought their drugs from their peers at school.

Now, let's examine the various categories of drugs which may be abused by our children.

NARCOTICS

Also known as opiates, many in this category of drugs have a legitimate medical use as a pain reliever, but also may create a high degree of dependence in the user, and thus become an abused drug. Common names of narcotics include opium, morphine, heroin and codeine, all of which are derived from the resin of the seed pod of the Asian poppy. Some synthesized or manufactured narcotics include meperidine.

Typically, opium is sold in dark brown chunks, or as a powder. The drug is usually smoked or eaten. Similarly, heroin may be in the form of a white or brown powder, which is then dissolved in water and injected. Heroin, which most experts acknowledge comprises 90 percent of the opiate abuse in the country, is often "cut" (dilluted) with sugar or quinine.

Opiate dependence is likely, particularly when the person uses large amounts of the drug, or even uses smaller amounts over an extended period of time. Tolerance to the drug also occurs, forcing the abuser to ingest more of the drug to achieve the same desired effects.

SEDATIVE-HYPNOTICS

Also known as depressants, this group of drugs depresses or slows down the body's metabolism. Again, many of these drugs have proper medical use as relaxants, calming down anxious people or prompting sleep. Typically known as tranquilizers, sleeping pills or sedatives, these drugs can cause both physical and psychological dependence.

Included in the sedative-hypnotic group are two major sub-categories, barbituates and benzodiazepines. Barbituates—often called "barbs" or "downers"—include amobarbital, pentobarbital, and secobarbital. All of these are available as capsules and tablets, and occasionally in a liquid form or in suppositories.

Benzodiazepines include the well-known tranquilizers diazepam (Valium), chlordiazepoxide (Librium) and chlorazepate (Tranxene), which are also sold as "downers" and also have a high dependency risk.

Methaqualone (Quaalude) is a sedative-hypnotic which is neither a barbituate nor a benzodiazepine. Its original medical use was as an anxiety-reliever and as a sleep aid; now, however, it has become one of the most commonly-abused drugs, and can cause both psychological and physical dependence.

A recent development in the sedative-hypnotic field is the creation of "look-alike" drugs which physically resemble and physiologically mimic actual sedative-hypnotics. These "look-alikes" contain over-the-counter drugs such as antihistamines and decongestants, which cause drowsiness.

STIMULANTS

This is the umbrella label for a wide variety of drugs that are used to increase mental alertness and physical activity. Millions of Americans ingest a stimulant—caffeine—daily in their coffee, soda or chocolate bars. Other well-known stimulants include amphetamines and cocaine.

Amphetamines may include three very similar drugs: amphetamine, destramphetamine and methamphetamine. On the street, amphetamines are known as "speed," "uppers," "bennies," "white crosses," and "crystal." The latter slang description stems from the fact that in their pure state, amphetamines are yellowish crystals which are then manufactured in tablet or capsule form. Other methods of ingestion include sniffing or injection.

Amphetamines have two basic medical uses: in the treatment of narcolepsy, which is a relatively rare disorder characterized by uncontrolled sleep episodes, and in the short-term treatment of obesity. Unfortunately, amphetamines may cause a psychological dependence, prompting users to abuse the drug to counteract the "down" feeling they get when its effect wears off.

As with sedative-hypnotics, "look-alikes" of amphetamines have recently become available. These usually contain varying amounts of three weak stimulants—caffeine, ephedrine and phenylpropanolamine—which are found in over-the-counter preparations, such as decongestants and diet pills.

To combat state regulations which were enacted to make "look-alikes" illegal, a new generation of drugs—known as "act-alikes"—has emerged. Chemically the same as "look-alikes," the drugs are simply shaped and colored so as not to resemble any prescription or over-the-counter drug. These "act-alikes" are touted to young people as legal and harmless (but virtually no drug, when abused, is harmless), and their abuse is mounting.

Caffeine, though not popularly considered as such, is a drug, and perhaps the most used drug in the world. In its pure form, it is a bitter, white, crystal-like substance which is found in cola, tea, cocoa and coffee. Caffeine is also in—sometimes surprisingly—other products, such as aspirin, non-prescription cough and cold remedies, soft drinks and diet pills.

The real danger of caffeine abuse comes not from drinking coffee (doses under 500–600 milligrams of caffeine, the amount found in about 4–6 cups of coffee, is considered relatively safe) but from the abuse of tablets containing caffeine.

Cocaine: This drug is extracted from the leaves of the coca plant and is one of the most dangerous, dependence-producing drugs the world knows. Cocaine is a central nervous system stimulant, and it is available in several different forms. The most popular form of the drug is cocaine hydrochloride, which is a fine white crystal-like powder, also available in larger pieces called "rocks." Cocaine is usually sniffed or injected, though there are two other methods of ingestion which are also extremely dangerous.

The first, freebasing, involves the conversion of cocaine into a purified, altered substance which is suitable for smoking. Comedian Richard Pryor nearly died from burns suffered while attempting to freebase cocaine. Its effects on the body, which will be explained in detail in the following chapter, are even more dangerous than normal cocaine because it reaches the brain quicker.

Crack is the second—and more worrisome—new form of cocaine to be introduced in the country. It is considered by experts to be the most addictive form of cocaine, which, researchers say, is the only drug laboratory animals will choose over food to the point of starving themselves to death.

How is crack made? Cocaine is mixed with baking soda and water, heated in a pot, dried and then broken into tiny rocks that are sold as crack. Typically, these are then smoked in glass pipes.

What makes crack so attractive to youths is its price: crack is usually available for as little as $10, so it's extremely affordable to most children. Crack is easy to use, either smoked in a pipe or rolled into a cigarette, and because its immediate effects dissipate within minutes after ingestion, crack can be used at almost any time of day, without the fear of detection.

We'll examine crack's effects and side effects in the next chapter, but it's important to realize now that crack is highly-addictive and, because it's so readily available and inexpensive, poses perhaps the most serious of drug problems to our youth.

HALLUCINOGENS

Though not in use as much today as in the '60s and early '70s, hallucinogens—also referred to as psychedelics—are dangerous drugs which are addictive and have adverse physical and psychological effects.

The most well-known of these psychedelic drugs are LSD, which is a manufactured substance, and mescaline, which occurs naturally in the peyote cactus.

LSD is created from lysergic acid, which is found in ergot, a fungus that grows on rye and other grains. Discovered in 1938, LSD remains today as one of the most powerful mood-altering chemicals known. Colorless, odorless and tasteless, LSD is sold in capsule or tablet forms, and, occasionally, as a liquid. The usual method of ingestion is orally, but it is sometimes injected.

Mescaline is usually smoked or swallowed in tablet or capsule form, and is not as powerful as LSD. Another hallucinogen, psilocybin, is derived from mushrooms and is sold in tablet or capsule form.

PCP (technically, phencyclidine) is sometimes referred to as an hallucinogen, but since it can also relieve pain and/or act as a stimulant, precise categorization of this drug is difficult.

However, angel dust—the street name for PCP—is nonetheless dangerous. Available as a pure-white crystal powder, a tablet or a capsule, angel dust can be ingested orally, smoked, sniffed or injected. A common method of smoking PCP involves sprinkling the powder on marijuana or parsley.

At one time after its development in the '50s, PCP was used medically as an anesthetic; however, it was withdrawn from the market after reports of hallucinations were made and attributed to the drug.

CANNABIS

The most well-known cannabis is marijuana, a drug derived from the cannabis sativa plant. A marijuana joint (cigarette) is made from the dried particles of the plant.

Though marijuana contains more than 400 chemicals, the main mind-altering ingredient is a substance known as THC (delta–9–tetrahydrocannabinol). Studies show that severe psychological damage can occur when marijuana contains two percent THC. Marijuana potency is dependent on a number of factors, including the type of plant, weather, soil and time of harvest, but today's marijuana is as much as ten times more powerful than the marijuana used in the early '70s. Additionally, it contains from four to six percent THC—or about double or triple the amount known to cause serious damage.

Long-term use of marijuana may produce a psychological dependency, but also worrisome are the physical effects, which are detailed in the next chapter. Marijuana is often the first drug (other than alcohol) tried by children, and the greater a person's involvement with marijuana, the greater the chances are that person will begin to use other drugs in conjunction with marijuana.

Hashish, or hash, is made from the resin of the leaves and flowers of the marijuana plant; the resin is pressed into cakes or slabs. Hash may contain five to ten times the amount of THC as marijuana, and hash oil may be up to 50 percent THC.

INHALANTS

These are breathable chemicals which are not often thought of as drugs, because they were never meant to be used in that manner. But they were found to emit mind-altering vapors, and have become drugs of abuse. Among the substances abused are model airplane glue, nail polish remover, cleaning fluids, lighter fluids and gasoline. Some aerosols—including paints, non-stick coating sprays and hair sprays—are also inhaled. Halothane, nitrous oxide (better known as laughing gas), amyl nitrite and butyl nitrite are other abused inhalants.

Amyl nitrite is typically packaged in cloth-covered, sealed bulbs which make a snapping sound when popped; consequently, they have earned the name "poppers" or "snappers." Medically, the drug is used for cardiac patients and for diagnostic purposes, because it dilates the blood vessels and quickens the heart rate. Since 1979, amyl nitrite has been available by prescription only. Butyl nitrite, known on the street as "rush" or "locker room," is usually packaged in small bottles.

Because inhalants are inexpensive, they are particularly attractive to young people seeking a high. Also, since many inhalants are found in everyday household supplies, a child often inadvertently misuses the product. Special care must be taken to make sure such substances are treated with the same respect as medicines, and kept out of the reach of children.

ALCOHOL

The abuse of alcohol is the most pervasive drug problem in the country today, with more than 70 percent of Americans using alcohol at one time or another.

Yet, very few Americans—particularly our youth—realize one inarguable fact about alcohol: it contains a poison. The chief ingredient in alcohol is methanol, a chemical so volatile it can be burned and used as a fuel. The task of eliminating this poison from the bloodstream falls to the liver; unfortunately, this organ is capable of filtering only one ounce of alcohol from the blood per hour, and is severely taxed by the strain of this process.

Often misunderstood is the amount of alcohol found in various beverages, including beer, wine and whiskey. Ask most people which of those three has more alcohol, and the response would likely be whiskey. Yet, the fact is that there are equal amounts of alcohol found in 1-1/2 ounces of whiskey, four ounces of wine and 12 ounces of beer.

Also somewhat confusing is the alcohol content, which is measured by proof; each proof of alcohol accounts for one-half percent of the liquid's overall volume. Therefore, a whiskey that is 90 proof has an alcohol content of 45 percent.

Over a period of time, the abuser can develop a psychological dependence to alcohol. And, with long-term, heavy use, a physical dependence may also develop.

Certainly, the statistics in this book's opening chapter reveal the depth of the drinking problem in our country. Besides the physical and psychological dangers imposed on our youth by alcohol, other occurrences—such as driving while intoxicated, and the combination of other drugs with alcohol—pose additional serious threats to our children's health and well being. These will be examined in depth in the following chapters.

ANABOLIC-ANDROGENIC STEROIDS

These substances are used most often by male high school athletes in an effort to increase muscle mass and strength. The basis of anabolic steroids is testosterone, a male sex hormone which allegedly causes nitrogen and protein to be retained in the body, which is then said to develop into muscle.

No well-designed scientific study has been able to verify these claims; those few research reports in medical journals which seem to support the claims can be shown to be either poorly controlled or not well-designed.

Actually, anabolic steroids may represent the ultimate example of the placebo effect. The user expects to increase his/her strength, and trains harder in anticipation of the results. Consequently, anabolic steroids create a self-fulfilling prophecy, not by any action on their part, but by more concentrated workouts on the part of the user.

The use of anabolic steroids, which are usually introduced through injections, is particularly dangerous to youngsters, for reasons detailed in the next chapter.

DMSO

DMSO (dimethyl sulfoxide) is a non-narcotic substance which has won mostly undeserved praise as a treatment for musculoskeletal injuries, and may be used by high school athletes. Actually an industrial solvent, DMSO is absorbed rapidly and almost completely through the skin, giving the user a garlic-like taste and odor in the mouth minutes after absorption. Typically, it is applied in gel or liquid form to the site of the injury. Not surprisingly, the majority of well-controlled medical studies have shown no tangible benefit from the use of DMSO.

NICOTINE

Nicotine is a toxic chemical which is found only in tobacco products, such as cigarettes, cigars, chewing tobacco and snuff. Though the consumption of cigarettes appears to be declining among our youth, the use of other tobacco products, such as chewing tobacco and snuff, needs to be addressed. Cases of oral cancer have been linked to the products, and that information must be shared with our children.

CHAPTER THREE

THE SHORT- AND LONG-TERM EFFECTS OF DRUGS

Every action in life carries with it consequences. We make decisions by weighing our understanding of consequences for a variety of options, and choose accordingly.

Unfortunately, young people often don't have the proper information, or appreciation, regarding the consequences of their actions. Experts speculate that one reason why teen suicide is so rampant is that its victims do not fully comprehend the finality of suicide; that they do not consider death as a consequence, but think they will somehow "wake up" to discover the problems which drove them to suicide have disappeared.

Obviously, the consequences of taking and abusing drugs are much less definite, particularly in the minds of young people, than the outcome of suicide. And since youths are imbued with a certain sense of invulnerability, the thought of developing physiological or psychological problems as the result of drug abuse is distant from their minds.

What is uppermost in their thoughts, however, is the immediate gratification supplied by the drug—the high, the lift, the feeling of euphoria. Also prevalent is the weighty peer pressure to try drugs or alcohol many teens experience.

Therefore, it is incumbent upon us to make certain our children know both the short- and long-term consequences of drug use. In a later chapter, we will examine the crucial role self esteem plays in our children's ability to resist peer pressure to try drugs. We also must inform them exactly how drugs work in their bodies, and what havoc is wreaked by them.

Here is a drug-by-drug look at what these substances do to the body.

NARCOTICS

Narcotics are taken for their relaxant effect on the user. When the drug is injected, the user feels an immediate rush, which is one of the addictive properties of the drug.

However, the drug also produces a variety of unpleasant side-effects, including restlessness, nausea and vomiting. The abuser may bounce dramatically from feeling alert to feeling drowsy, and is unable to control, or predict, these swings. When large doses are ingested, the user cannot be awakened, the pupils shrink, and the skin becomes cold, moist and bluish.

In the event of an overdose, convulsions and coma may result, and breathing may become slow and shallow, to the point of death.

Long-term use of the drug may lead to infections in the heart lining and valves, skin abscesses, and congested lungs. Additionally, a very real danger of developing AIDS (acquired immune deficiency syndrome) is present because narcotics are usually injected via a needle; the use of unsterile needles is a leading cause of AIDS, which must be considered a potential side-effect of narcotics abuse.

The user quickly falls into dependence on the drug, and, as his/her tolerance level increases, so does the amount of the drug needed to achieve the same high.

Pregnant women who abuse opiates run even stronger health risks. Nearly half of these women develop anemia, heart disease, diabetes, pneumonia, or hepatitis during pregnancy and childbirth. Additionally, they suffer a higher rate of spontaneous abortions, breech deliveries, caesarean sections, premature births and stillbirths.

Most tragically, infants born to such women often experience painful withdrawal symptoms from narcotics, for up to several months. And often, babies of opiate-dependent women die soon after birth.

It's important to point out these pregnancy risks to our young girls, because that knowledge serves as a further warning against the development of an addiction to narcotics. Remember, though the pregnancy issue may not be an immediate concern to young girls now (though the teenage pregnancy rate is extremely high), remind them that an addiction which begins during their teenage years could carry through their childbearing years. The best way to cure an addiction is to prevent it before it begins.

SEDATIVE/HYPNOTICS

Used as an aid to relieve anxiety or promote sleep, this category of drugs works by slowing the body's functions. These drugs can result in physical and/or psychological dependency, and regular use over an extended period of time may lead to increased tolerance of the drug.

With barbituates, there is a fine line between the dosage that produces sleep and the amount that kills. That reality is best—and most dramatically—illustrated by the fact that barbituate overdose is a factor in one-third of all reported drug-related deaths.

In lesser doses, barbituates still can cause slurred speech, staggering walk, poor judgment and slow, unsteady reflexes. Consequently, the affected individual is not suited to drive a car or operate machinery, and creates a dangerous situation—for himself and others—while doing so.

Other possible effects of overdose include shallow breathing, dilated pupils, a weak, rapid pulse, cold and clammy skin, coma—and, as already mentioned, death.

Dependence—both physical and psychological—to depressants is intense, and the body does build a tolerance to the drugs, demanding an increasing amount to achieve the same "high." Withdrawal from barbituates, for example, is often considered to be more serious than heroin withdrawal.

The combination of any sedative-hypnotic drug with alcohol is a particularly dangerous one. Alcohol also tends to slow the body's functions; when taken in conjunction with sedative-hypnotics, the drugs' effects are magnified and the risk of death greatly increases. This is effect is known as "potentiation;" in this instance, one drug plus one drug does not equal the effect of two drugs, but of three.

These drugs, when abused by pregnant women, can cause harm to the unborn fetus, and may, in fact, cause the baby to be born with a physical dependency on the drug.

Other symptoms include breathing difficulties, irregular and disturbed sleep, sweating, irritability, and fever.

Additionally, sedative-hypnotics have been shown to cause birth defects and/or behavioral problems in babies born to mothers who abused the drugs during pregnancy.

The side-effects of methaqualone (often known as "ludes") are somewhat similar to the other sedative drugs. A person's judgment may be impaired because of the drug, or drowsiness may result, making the individual susceptible to accidents. Other possible effects include convulsion, coma, and death by overdose.

STIMULANTS

Though cocaine and crack are technically considered stimulants, their importance is broad enough to warrant individual sections on each. In this analysis of the side effects of stimulants, we will focus upon amphetamines and caffeine.

Within about a half-hour of the ingestion of about two cups of coffee (about 150–300 milligrams of caffeine), a person begins to realize the effects of the drug. The body's metabolism, temperature and blood pressure may increase, as may the urine output and blood sugar levels. Other effects include hand tremors, a loss of appetite and coordination, and delayed or difficult sleep.

Extremely high doses of caffeine—by the ingestion of tablets containing larger doses of the drug—may cause nausea, diarrhea, trembling, headache, nervousness and sleeplessness.

Poisonous doses of caffeine are marked by convulsions, breathing failure and death; however, it's virtually impossible for death to occur from drinking coffee or tea, and such poisonous amounts are usually ingested through tablets.

Tolerance to the drug, however, may build up with the use of about four-to-six cups of coffee a day. With that tolerance may come a craving for the drug, manifested by a person's need to "have that morning cup of coffee." Additionally, some report withdrawal-like symptoms when they suddenly stop using caffeine, including headaches, irritability and mood changes.

Amphetamines act quickly and dramatically on the body. Their job is to stimulate the body's metabolism, and that occurs immediately: heart and breathing rates increase, pupils dilate and appetite decreases. The abuser may also have a dry "cotton" mouth, unexplained sweating, headache, dizziness, nausea, insomnia, blurred vision and anxiety.

Overdoses of the drug render the abuser flush and/or pale, with a rapid, or irregular, heartbeat. Other effects of an overdose may include loss of coordination and a physical collapse.

Psychologically, the user may feel anxious and restless, and may experience abrupt mood swings.

Long-term physical abuse of stimulants may lead to malnutrition, skin disorders, ulcers and diseases stemming from vitamin deficiencies. The abuser will also suffer from a lack of sleep, experience weight loss and have bouts of depression. Frequent large doses have been known to produce brain damage, causing speech and thought difficulties. Psychological effects of long-term use include the possible development of amphetamine psychosis, a condition in which the person sees, hears and feels things that do not exist (hallucinations); has irrational thoughts (delusions) and suffers from paranoia. At this stage of addiction, the abuser frequently exhibits bizarre, and sometimes violent, behavior.

Special threats surface when the abuser injects the stimulants. An amphetamine injection prompts a sudden, dramatic increase in blood pressure that can cause death from stroke, high fever, or heart failure.

Also, injection carries with it the possibility of infection, either from unsterile needles or contaminated solutions. The most well-known of the possible consequences from injection is AIDS; other infections can cause lung or heart disease, kidney damage, stroke, or problems with other tissues and blood vessels. Deaths have been known to occur as a result of these effects.

Though amphetamines probably don't create a physical dependence in most people, psychological dependence is high. Tolerance is also quickly developed, which prompts the abuser to take larger quantities of the drug.

Withdrawal from amphetamines is difficult: possible effects include fatigue, long sleeping jags, irritability, hunger and depression.

Though not as strong as amphetamines, their "look-alike" and "act-alike" counterparts, when taken in large quantities, also may cause anxiety, difficult breathing, rapid heartbeat, and an overall weakness. One dramatic result of an overdose of these "alike" drugs is severe high blood pressure, which may lead to cerebral hemorrhaging and death.

Also, if an abuser accidentally or purposely takes a similar dosage of actual amphetamines as (s)he might of the "alike" drugs, an overdose might result. Additionally, the abuse of "alike" drugs can lead a person to harder, more dangerous substances.

COCAINE

Often called the "champagne of drugs," cocaine imparts a severely high psychological dependency on those who abuse it. The effects of cocaine peak about 20 minutes after the drug is snorted through the nose, and dissipate after about an hour or two. Cocaine, as a stimulant, increases alertness and creates a sense of euphoria, which is the hook which creates the high degree of psychological dependence.

Immediate physical effects include dilated pupils and elevations in heart rate, breathing rate and body temperature.

Freebasing—the smoking of cocaine—prompts a shorter, more intense high, but also causes increased risks, including confusion, slurred speech, anxiety and psychological problems.

Crack is even more addictive than cocaine because it produces an almost immediate, intense high in a matter of seconds. However, the devastating low that follows within a few minutes usually leaves the abuser craving more crack.

The short-term physical effects of crack are the same as cocaine, only more intense. It elevates heart and blood pressure, which could lead to arrythmia or a heart attack, and may cause abusers to feel as if bugs are crawling over their skin.

The continued abuse of cocaine in any form may lead to feelings of restlessness, irritability, anxiety, and sleeplessness. Severe psychological problems, including paranoia or cocaine psychosis—hallucinations of touch, sight, taste, or smell—may also result.

Physical effects of snorting cocaine include a stuffy or runny nose, and long-term snorting can ulcerate the mucous membrane of the nose. Smoking cocaine may lead to emphysema and the increased risk of death due to the intensity of the high. Freebasing, because it often involves the use of volatile solvents, carries with it the added risk of explosion or fire. And injecting cocaine can lead to AIDS or other communicable diseases passed by nonsterile needles and contaminated solutions.

And, of course, as evidenced by the deaths of Len Bias and Don Rogers, cocaine can kill at any time.

HALLUCINOGENS

Though hallucinogens are not used as widely today as during the '60s and early '70s, some officials are reporting a surge in popularity in these drugs, particularly LSD. Perhaps the renewed interest in the drug stems from a lapse in memory regarding the ill effects—both short- and long-term—of LSD. This section will serve as a reminder of those negative results.

Effects of psychedelics vary from person to person. In fact, the drug has different results depending on the user's personality, mood, expectations and environment.

Mentally, LSD affects a person's emotions, causing rapid mood swings. The abuser may seem to experience several emotions at once, and may feel as if (s)he "hears" colors or "sees" sounds. These "bad trips," as they're called in drug parlance, can be frightening and cause anxiety and panic. Other symptoms of these negative experiences include confusion, suspiciousness, feelings of helplessness and loss of control. Several instances have been recorded in which abusers had no comprehension of their limitations and attempted to fly out windows, only to fall to their deaths. Additionally, the abuser may be subject to flashbacks, in which (s)he experiences the drug's ill effects without having ingested the drug.

Physically, LSD and other psychedelic drugs, such as mescaline, cause increased body temperature, heart rate and blood pressure, dilated pupils, sweating, appetite loss, sleeplessness, dry mouth and tremors. Death from an overdose is also a possibility.

Heavy use of hallucinogens may cause impaired memory, an abbreviated attention span, difficulty with abstract thinking and overall mental confusion. It is not yet known if these symptoms dissipate after LSD is no longer ingested. Also not yet fully determined is the exact degree of psychological dependence an abuser develops on hallucinogens; it is known, however, that the body does build a tolerance to the drug, and requires more of it to achieve the desired results.

PCP

PCP (phencyclidine) is known popularly as angel dust, a powerful drug which causes hallucinations. Once ingested, PCP increases the abuser's heart rate and blood pressure, and causes sweating, unsteadiness, numbness and flushing. Large doses of the drug can result in drowsiness, convulsions and coma, as well as heart and lung failure, or ruptured blood vessels in the brain.

Those who use PCP are unable to precisely describe its effects on them. It may act as a stimulant for some, while, for others, it changes their perception of themselves and their environment. Almost always affected are speech, muscle coordination and vision, and senses of touch and pain are dulled.

Chronic use of PCP can affect an abuser's memory, perception, concentration and judgment, and cause paranoia, an aura of invulnerability and angst. Either aggression or a difficulty in communicating may also result. Other effects of long-term use may include memory and speech impairments, and hearing voices or sounds which do not exist.

What may be most dangerous about PCP, however, is the violent or bizarre behavior exhibited by otherwise-normal people who are under its influence. Such behavior can cause death by drowning, burns, falls and automotive accidents.

MARIJUANA

Marijuana may very well be the most popular illegal drug in America. Though it's composed of more than 400 chemicals, marijuana has as its primary mind-altering ingredient THC (delta-9-tetrahydrocannabinol). The amount of THC determines how strong marijuana's effects will be.

Typically, marijuana is rolled into cigarettes, called joints, and smoked. Almost immediately, the abuser's heart beats faster, his pulse rate quickens, and he gets a dry mouth and throat. The heart rate may quicken by as much as 50 percent, depending on the potency of the marijuana. This can, in people with a poor blood supply to the heart, cause chest pain.

Some people have trouble remembering events that happened while high, and experience difficulty in performing functions that require concentration, rapid reactions and coordination, such as driving a car.

In fact, tests show that a person, after smoking marijuana, has impaired ability to perform a wide variety of functions normally associated with driving a car, such as staying in lane through curves, maintaining speed, and judging proper distance between cars. Reflexes are slowed and judgment is impaired. And these negative effects linger for up to six hours after the joint has been smoked—long after the high has subsided. Mixing alcohol with marijuana only further deteriorates a person's reflexes and functions.

Worrisome, too, is the fact that THC, the active ingredient in marijuana, is difficult for the body to purge. THC is absorbed by most tissues and organs when marijuana is smoked, but is stored primarily in fat. In an effort to eliminate THC from its system, the body transforms the substance into metabolites. These metabolites can be detected in urine tests for up to a week after a joint has been smoked, and in radioactive tests performed with animals, for up to a month.

Marijuana smoke, which contains about 2,000 chemicals, is considered to be harmful to the lungs, particularly since many abusers often inhale the smoke deeply and hold it in their lungs as long as possible. Some of the ingredients in marijuana are known to cause emphysema. And since many marijuana abusers also smoke cigarettes, the combined effects of the two substances further heighten health risks.

The possibility of cancer is another serious consideration for the marijuana abuser. Marijuana smoke has more known carcinogens (cancer-causing agents) than tobacco smoke. Metaplasia—cellular changes which are considered to be precursors of cancer—have been found in human tissue which has been exposed to marijuana smoke for a long period of time. Additionally, the tar from marijuana smoke has caused tumors on animal skin.

Evidence also exists that marijuana negatively affects the human reproductive system, causing irregular menstrual cycles in women and a temporary loss of fertility in both men and women. Also, it's been shown to influence the levels of some hormones which relate to sexuality. Unfortunately, marijuana may be most potent on the reproductive system when the user is an adolescent, since this is a time of physical and sexual development and maturation. Those who have smoked "grass" while pregnant have had low birthweight and premature babies.

Marijuana has some other serious side-effects on a young person's future. Firstly, it impairs a student's verbal and mathematical skills and ability to think and read with comprehension. Also, marijuana use by young people has been associated with a concurrent decline in interest in schoolwork. And marijuana sometimes opens the door for young people to begin experimenting with other drugs.

Psychological side-effects include acute panic anxiety reaction, in which the abuser feels he is losing all control. This panic usually subsides within a few hours.

Those who use marijuana over extended periods of time may develop a psychological dependence to the drug, and the body's tolerance for the drug may increase.

Another ill effect of marijuana is "burnout," which is the result of extended use of marijuana. Those suffering from burnout become dull, slow moving and inattentive—sometimes to the point of being unaware of their friends and surroundings.

Besides alcohol, marijuana is the leading "peer" drug in our nation. It's important to reinforce our children's self-esteem and arm them with proper information to help them resist the peer pressure—and say no.

INHALANTS

These are especially dangerous because they are usually located within easy reach around the house. Remember, whether the inhalants are abused intentionally or unintentionally, the effects and risks are the same. Take all necessary precautions to keep such dangerous substances either out of easy access, or out of your house entirely.

Inhalants work by slowing down the body's functions, much as an anesthetic would. Consequently, at low doses, the abuser may feel slightly stimulated; at greater amounts, they may lose inhibitions and control. And at high doses, the abuser can lose consciousness.

Using inhalants can also cause some unpleasant—and rather rapid—physical side effects, including nausea, coughing, sneezing, dizziness, lack of coordination and lack of appetite. Sniffing solvents and aerosols can impair judgment and slow the body's heart and breathing rate. The potency of these effects depends on a variety of factors, such as what specific substance is inhaled, and in what quantity, and on the metabolism and personality of the abuser.

Continued abuse of inhalants can cause a person to lose perspective of his surroundings, dwindle his self-control, prompt violent (and uncharacteristic) behavior and unconsciousness. If a person vomits while unconscious, it's possible to die from aspiration.

Highly concentrated amounts of solvents or aerosol sprays, when sniffed, can cause death. Concentrated sniffing of virtually any inhalant (when sniffed from a paper bag, for example) displaces the oxygen in the lungs, or slows down the breathing rate so much until breathing stops, and can cause death.

Over an extended period of abuse, inhalants can cause permanent damage to the central nervous system, muscle fatigue, salt imbalance and weight loss. The long-term use of some inhalants may damage certain organs, including the liver and kidneys, and have adverse effects on blood and bone marrow.

As with many other drugs, the body builds a tolerance to inhalants, which forces the user to sniff greater amounts more frequently to get high.

The combination of sniffing inhalants and using other drugs that act as a sedative on the body, such as tranquilizers or alcohol, is particularly dangerous and may result in loss of consciousness, coma or even death.

Inhalants are one of the few drugs of abuse which are legally found in almost every home in America. Special care must be taken—by adults and children—to avoid the inadvertent breathing of their fumes. When working with such products (labels on the outside of these products carry warnings about the inhaling of the fumes), be sure to do so in a well-ventilated area.

ANABOLIC-ANDROGENIC STEROIDS

Those who use anabolic steroids—primarily young athletes seeking to build muscle bulk and strength—are inviting short and long-term dangers to their bodies. Even when prescribed by doctors in low therapeutic doses, anabolic steroids carry grave consequences. Sterility, loss of libido, weight gain and enlargement of the prostate gland are just some of the adverse side-effects of the drug. Liver cancer has resulted from anabolic steroid therapy, as has heart disease, stroke and peripheral vascular problems.

Since those abusing steroids may ingest from five to 15 times the amount of a therapeutic dose, the drug's side effects are likely to develop more quickly—and more intensely.

Prepubescent athletes are caused serious problems by the drug. Young girls who use anabolic steroids experience such undesirable side effects as masculinization, excessive hair growth and disruption of normal body growth patterns. Unfortunately, most of these consequences are irreversible.

Also irreversible is the premature closure of the epiphyseal plates—the growth areas—of long bones which occurs in young males who take anabolic steroids. Consequently, a person who abuses anabolic steroids while still growing will likely never attain his or her full natural height.

DMSO

What must be remembered about DMSO—dimethyl sulfoxide—is that it was originally developed as an industrial solvent. Again, used mostly by athletes to treat musculoskeletal injuries, DMSO has not yet been conclusively proven effective for that purpose.

However, the drug's side effects have been well-documented, and include nausea, headache, diarrhea, localized skin rashes, painful urination and possible severe allergic reaction.

NICOTINE

In its purest form, nicotine is one of the most toxic of all poisons. Found primarily in the leaves of the tobacco plant, nicotine is introduced to the body either through the lung membrane (when smoking a cigarette), the mucosa of the mouth (when chewing tobacco) or through the stomach and intestines (once the juices are swallowed). Spitting the juices out does not significantly reduce the amount of nicotine absorbed.

Nicotine is habit forming, and has been associated with many health problems, such as cancer, and cardiovascular and respiratory diseases. Those who use smokeless tobacco for extended periods of time run a 50 times greater risk of developing cancer of the gums and mouth which, at best, is disfiguring and, at worst, can kill.

Certainly, the case against cigarettes, cigars and pipe-smoking has been well-documented by the Surgeon General of the United States. However, many—including medical professionals—are of the wrong opinion that smokeless tobacco is harmless. Studies show that it is extremely dangerous.

Be certain to steer your child away from all tobacco-related products, including chewing tobacco and snuff.

CONCLUSION

Many of the ill effects of the drugs described in this section are redundant, because the body tends to act in certain ways when foreign substances are introduced to it. What's important to remember is this: virtually any abuse of any drug—one time or 1,000 times—can lead to physical and/or psychological dependence, illness and even death. That is not meant to scare you or your children, just to give you the knowledge you need to know to weigh the consequences of drugs.

Too many promising young people—Len Bias, Janis Joplin, John Belushi—thought "one more high" wouldn't hurt them.

Instead, it killed them.

Next chapter: we'll study alcohol and its impact on the body.

CHAPTER FOUR

ALCOHOL AND ITS EFFECTS

Unlike many of the drugs discussed in the previous chapter, alcohol is legal. In fact, it has been ingrained into the very fabric of our society as a means of celebration. We drink toasts at weddings and banquets; we invite members of the opposite sex to "have a drink" as a means of acquaintance; on special holidays, such as Christmas and Thanksgiving, liquor is poured to mark the occasion.

We drink to celebrate, to reminisce, to forget, to dream. Alcohol has become a focal point in the social lives of millions of Americans. It's no wonder that our young people are in such a rush—and have such intensity—to try alcohol.

Ironically, if alcohol were a new drug attempting to gain approval from the Food and Drug Administration today, it would likely be banned. It contributes to the loss of hundreds of thousands of lives each year, costs the country millions of dollars in lost productivity, shreds the dreams and careers of too many Americans, and turns thousands of families into a shambles.

Yet, alcohol is with us, most likely to stay. But before our teens can make responsible decisions on whether or not to drink, they must first be given information on the ill consequences of alcohol. Armed with that knowledge, the young person can make the decision to drink responsibly, or perhaps not drink at all.

First of all, alcohol has no nutritive value at all, but does contain about 150 calories per shot (about 1-1/2 oz.) of liquor. Besides having no minerals, vitamins or proteins, alcohol inhibits the digestive system, and may rob the body of necessary nutrients.

Most of us know the feeling a drink or two provides: less inhibition, slightly relaxed, and slightly euphoric. This kind of limited "social" drinking, if not constant, seems to cause no direct harm. One of the problems with teen drinkers, however, is an apparent inability to limit themselves to just one or two drinks; additionally, even "just one or two" drinks may be enough to impair judgment and reactions, and contribute to traffic accidents.

For example, ingesting one drink (1-1/2 oz. of alcohol, which is the equivalent of a shot of 86-proof liquor, one 12-oz. can of beer or a four-ounce glass of wine) in an hour rarely affects responsible driving. Two drinks in the same time period, however, begins raising the blood alcohol content to about .05 percent, which is near the "danger zone" of responsible driving. Three to four drinks in an hour pushes the blood alcohol level to near .09 percent, which means the driver is driving while impaired. Five to six drinks in a 60-minute period raises the blood alcohol level to .10 percent and above—which is above most states' legal limit for sober driving.

Additionally, since alcohol is, in reality, a poison, it adversely affects the body from the first sip. For example, brain damage occurs with each ingestion of alcohol; admittedly, the damage, with limited intake of alcohol, is negligible, but alcoholics and those who frequently drink large volumes of liquor suffer deeper brain damage, which is irreversible.

Alcohol, contrary to what many people believe, is a depressant, not a stimulant. As a depressant, it slows down the body's functions. With the ingestion of three to four drinks an hour, the person will suffer impaired speech and coordination, diminished inhibitions and a loss of judgment. More than that amount ingested in an hour, and the effects become even more pronounced: slurred words, staggered gait, unpredictable emotions, mood swings, and inappropriate behavior. Also, the drinker's perception of his reaction time is impaired, so he may think his senses are alert when, in reality, they're not.

What most youths—and adults—fail to appreciate is that when someone is drunk, that person has, in reality, overdosed on a drug. In this case, the drug is alcohol.

Particularly dangerous is the ingestion of alcohol in concert with other drugs, especially depressants. It falls to the liver to filter out the alcohol and depressants from the bloodstream. The poison—alcohol—is removed first, leaving the downers to be reabsorbed in the intestines. This lingering prolongs and intensifies (up to three times) the effect of the downers, and is known as potentiation. Therefore, the combination of alcohol and depressants can lead to serious illness, or even death.

The liver can only filter about an ounce of alcohol from the blood per hour, and is quite taxed by the strain. A consequence is cirrhosis of the liver, which is irreversible and one of the most well-known effects of alcohol abuse. In fact, about 85 percent of all deaths attributed to cirrhosis of the liver are related to alcohol. Additionally, alcohol has also been named as a causative factor in liver cancer.

The heart is susceptible to the effects of alcohol abuse, too. Abnormalities in heart rhythm and pumping action may occur, and may be life-threatening.

Also threatened by overuse of alcohol is normal brain function. Abusers may have trouble thinking clearly and may, with continued abuse, suffer blackouts, which are periods of time which cannot be recalled by the user.

Other side effects include the inhibition of the synthesis of glucose, which forces the body to tap its supply of glycogen in the liver. Once that store is depleted, hypoglycemia (low blood sugar) results.

Prolonged and extreme use of alcohol may cause psychological and/or physical dependency. Withdrawal symptoms from those trying to quit the drug are extreme: body tremors, severe sleep difficulties, digestive problems and delerium tremens (shakes, disorientation and hallucinations).

Alcohol is known to cause problems in pregnancy, too, and can cause Fetal Alcohol Syndrome (FAS), a collection of birth abnormalities. Although it is not known for certain how much alcohol is too much, researchers say that as little as a few ounces of hard liquor (three beers, glasses of wine, or shots) during the first trimester of pregnancy can cause FAS.

Quite simply, when the mother drinks, so does the baby. And the drink the baby receives is in the same concentration as the one the mother takes. Alcohol passes directly through the placenta to the fetus. However, the fetus's immature organs are not able to break down the alcohol as quickly, or as thoroughly, as that of an adult. As a result, the alcohol interferes with or damages the developing organs and tissues of the fetus.

Since the fetus is most vulnerable during the first trimester, consumption of alcohol during this time may have the most damaging effects, including gross birth defects and severe mental retardation. Consumption of alcohol during the second and third trimesters can result in abnormally low birth weight and height, as well as hyperactivity and a lack of normal motor control, which manifests itself later in the youngster's life.

The fetal brain is the organ most likely to be affected by alcohol. FAS babies, abnormally small at birth, are born with exceptionally small heads. Some babies have undersized brains and show signs of mental deficiency. These youngsters may never catch up to normal growth, and evidence shows that their IQs may not improve with age.

FAS babies may have narrow eyes and low nasal bridges with short, upturned noses. Some are jittery and have poor coordination, short attention spans and behavioral problems. They may also have facial or limb malformations, cleft palate, or suffer from heart or kidney problems.

Obviously, not every FAS baby has all of these defects. And some have a less severe form of FAS, known as fetal alcohol effects, or modified FAS. Typically, these defects don't manifest themselves until the child is older. These children may suffer from one or more of the following: hyperactivity, lack of concentration, behavioral problems in school, below-normal weight and abnormal sleeping patterns.

50 TEENAGE ALCOHOLISM AND SUBSTANCE ABUSE

In some cases, doctors observed that babies born to alcoholic mothers were themselves alcoholics. The babies suffered from early stages of liver disease and went through the classic symptoms of alcohol withdrawal during the one to two weeks necessary to wean them from alcohol. Other newborns were noted to be nervous, cranky and experienced tremors, all signs of withdrawal symptoms.

The potential ill effects of alcohol to the baby continue if the mother chooses to consume alcohol and nurse her newborn. Many nursing mothers are told that drinking a glass of wine or beer before breastfeeding will help relax them and start the flow of milk. Now, it is believed that alcohol may actually cause a reduction in the milk supply. And since alcohol enters the breast milk at the same level as it enters the mother's bloodstream, the nursing infant may suffer from pseudo-Cushing syndrome, characterized by easy bruising, and a "moon" or "balloon" face. Long term effects are not yet known.

Therefore, it's imperative for our teens (males, too: some research indicates alcohol has a detrimental effect on a man's sperm) to learn to be able to discipline—and limit—themselves regarding alcohol. Teenagers who learn to control their alcoholic intake are more likely to be responsible drinkers as adults.

CHAPTER FIVE

THE WARNING SIGNS OF SUBSTANCE ABUSE

"How can I know if my child is abusing drugs or alcohol?" That question is one of the most-often asked by parents in an effort to help them recognize signs of substance abuse by their children. Certainly, the best time to prevent such abuse is before it begins. However, even in the best of situations—with the most loving, attentive, supportive parents—some children still fall prey, for any number of reasons, to substance abuse.

In those instances, it's crucial to detect the abuse as quickly as possible, so that professional help can be brought in and the teenager helped. Nearly all professionals agree that substance abuse is a problem more easily confronted and handled in its early stages, before the individual has built up a strong psychological and/or physical dependence to the drug.

How, then, can you know if your child is abusing drugs or alcohol? Unfortunately, there are only two definite ways to determine that: either the child tells you of his problem, or you catch your teenager high, inebriated, or in the process of abusing drugs or alcohol.

But, there are signs which may indicate your child is having trouble with substance abuse. Remember, these are only signs, and are by no means definite indications a person is involved with drugs or alcohol; only that (s)he MAY be.

The best way to detect if your child is using drugs or drinking excessively is to keep in touch with him/her. Talk with your teenager. Observe his/her friends. Discuss interests, activities, upcoming events.

And, importantly, listen to what your teen is saying, or not saying. Adolescence is a difficult time, often marked by periods of loneliness and uncertainty. It's a time of enormous peer pressure, of wanting to belong, of yearning to be one of the group. The resultant peer pressure is what prompts many teenagers to try that first drink or smoke that first joint. A few minutes of attentive conversation and listening each day will help you to know your teen better—and alert you to any possible problems that may need your intervention.

Though each drug has its own set of signs which indicate its use, there are many characteristics which are common to the abuse of all drugs. Here's a discussion on those particular warning signals:

ABRUPT CHANGE IN ATTENDANCE AT SCHOOL

Your child has rarely missed a day of school, and, in the past, has battled with you to attend school even when sick. Suddenly, (s)he's missing school frequently—sometimes, without your knowledge. And perhaps offers no further explanation other than, "I just don't feel right."

Be alert, too, for incidences of skipped classes during the school day. For example, if you receive a call saying your teen is missing only certain classes, that may be a warning signal. Similarly, if your child goes to school regularly, but has received several tardy notices—though you know (s)he leaves in ample time to arrive before school starts—that also may be a warning sign.

A DECLINE IN GRADES

Many teens fluctuate somewhat in academic performances, which is usually not indicative of substance abuse. What you should be on the lookout for, instead, is a dramatic decline: an A student is suddenly a C student, or a B student is now flunking most courses.

Such a decline—specifically when coupled with a poor attitude ("What do grades mean anyway? I really don't care about them") may reflect a substance abuse problem.

DISCIPLINE PROBLEMS

Again, the key here is to look for the deviation from your teen's regular behavior. If, suddenly, your child becomes a severe discipline problem at school—when before (s)he rarely had such difficulties—then this could be symptomatic of other problems, including substance abuse. A similar breakdown in discipline at home may also be cause for concern. Remember, though, that a certain amount of rebelliousness is characteristic of adolescence. Therefore, as is the case with many of these warning signals, discipline problems alone are not strong indicators of substance abuse. However, the combination of such problems with, for example, poor school attendance and declining grades, should alert you to the presence of some kind of problem—substance abuse or otherwise.

DETERIORATION OF PHYSICAL CONDITION

Long hours of sleep are typical of teenagers, usually to the chagrin of their parents, and alone are certainly not a positive indication of substance abuse. Instead, look for other changes in your child's condition—less stamina, or an uncharacteristic unwillingness to participate in family games or contests. If your teen is an athlete and on a high school sports team, a decline in interest in the sport could also signal the beginning of a problem.

Watch, too, for changes in the way your teen dresses. Don't view your teen's apparel with a fashion eye, but watch for sloppiness that is unusual for him/her. If a teenage girl, for example, who once was fastidious about her hair, suddenly doesn't even bother to run a brush through her hair in the morning, that could be indicative of a growing problem with drugs or alcohol.

UNCHARACTERISTIC TEMPER TANTRUMS

Few teenagers don't have loud arguments with their parents. That argumentative attitude is as much a part of adolescence, for many teens, as pimples and cracking voices.

So, it shouldn't be a source of concern if your teen argues with you. Be somewhat worried, however, if your teen suddenly begins throwing uncharacteristic—and unwarranted—temper tantrums. If the youth becomes uncontrollably angry over a relatively innocuous situation—such as what's for dinner—and such tantrums are coupled with two or more of the other signs, then trouble of some kind may be brewing.

This particular warning sign is one of the most difficult for parents to evaluate, because the teen is going through a series of changes, anyway, and parents are confused whether or not the temper tantrums are a part of growing up, or are symptomatic of another problem. Most experts feel that in and of themselves, the tantrums are usually not indicative of a substance abuse problem. But tantrums, in concert with several other instances of uncharacteristic behavior, may be.

OVERBEARING PROTECTION OF ROOM AND OTHER PERSONAL POSSESSIONS

Again, this is a tough signal to evaluate, primarily because teens generally want more and more privacy as they advance through adolescence. What you should be watchful for, however, is any overt concern a teen has for his/her belongings: locking the bedroom door to keep you out, for example. Certainly, teens have a right to privacy; it's when a child doesn't want you in his/her room—under any circumstances—that may be cause for concern.

Similarly, an uncharacteristic reluctance to discuss where (s)he is going, or with whom, may be another signal.

WEARING SUNGLASSES OR LONG-SLEEVED GARMENTS IN INAPPROPRIATE WEATHER

Donning sunglasses on a cold, dark, winter day is not appropriate and may be an effort to mask one of the most overt physical effects of alcohol or other drugs—bloodshot eyes. Similarly, wearing a long-sleeved shirt in hot, humid weather, may be an attempt to hide injection marks on the arm. These particular signs should be addressed right away, as outlined in Chapter 7.

UNUSUAL BORROWING OF MONEY

If your teen is continually asking for advances on an allowance, or borrows money despite having a job and low expenses, (s)he may be using the money to purchase drugs. In more desperate instances, the youth may steal items which can be pawned or sold. Certainly, that is one of the most serious signs of potential substance abuse.

CHANGE IN USUAL GROUP OF FRIENDS

While teens may experience vast changes in friends as they proceed through adolescence, often there remains a common friend throughout the shuffle. For example, a teen may "hang around" with a group of four or five, but then breakaway, with another member of the group, to another circle of friends. Then, the youth may again change groups, perhaps with another friend from the second group. In other words, there's usually somewhat of a continuity among friends and groups of friends.

But if your child suddenly begins running with an entirely different group of peers, that may signal something's amiss.

Pay particular heed if your teen, when asked about one or two previous "best friends," responds, "He's not cool," or "She's weird," or with similar expressions. Also, if members of the new group of friends dress inappropriately for the weather—as outlined above—that is another factor that may be indicative your teen is running with the "wrong crowd."

CHANGE IN FREQUENCY IN TRIPS TO BATHROOM OR OTHER 'PRIVATE PLACE'

Again, a tough determination, particularly since teens—at least according to their parents—may spend lifetimes in the bathroom. But the key here is frequency, rather than length of stay. Any dramatic change in frequency in trips to rooms or other locations where privacy is assured—such as an outside storage shed, a room in the basement, etc.—should be watched closely. The youth could be using those sites to ingest the drugs or alcohol.

PRESENCE OF DRUG PARAPHERNALIA

Such items as rolling papers, pipes, matches (if your teen does not smoke cigarettes), "bongs" or other instruments are strong signs of possible drug abuse.

UNEXPLAINED ABSENCES OF LIQUOR IN THE HOUSE

Dwindling levels of liquor in bottles—or the disappearance of entire bottles—could be a strong sign of an alcohol problem with some member of the family. Try to check any liquor in your house periodically—about once a month—and watch for any dramatic and unaccountable discrepancies in supply. Many parents opt to keep the liquor under lock and key, or to not keep any in the house at all.

Certainly, no parents want to believe their children are abusing drugs or alcohol. But statistics tell us millions are, and parents—besides being the first line of defense for children against substance abuse—are also the ones who should be able to recognize possible warning signs of such abuse, and get appropriate help.

Again, you must remember that most of these signs, when manifested alone, do not usually indicate any kind of problem, other than the general woes of adolescence. It's the combination of two or three of these signs that should cause worry—and even then, signs themselves are not conclusive proof that your child is abusing alcohol or drugs. But an accumulation of such signs is usually proof positive that some kind of problem—perhaps not abuse, but an adjustment problem, or a lack of self-esteem—is present.

Here, however, are signs that may be indicative of abuse of particular drugs:

COCAINE (CRACK, AND OTHER STIMULANTS, SUCH AS AMPHETAMINES)

The signs of stimulant abuse include:
—dilated pupils. The abuser may try to hide this condition by constantly wearing sunglasses or other dark glasses;
—uncharacteristic activity, irritability, nervousness or aggression. Remember, stimulants speed up the body's

function, and the abuser may have trouble sitting still, remaining inactive, or controlling his/her temper;
—"cotton" mouth. The abuser may drink inordinate amounts of water to satiate thirst, and may be constantly licking his/her lips;
—"sniffling". Constant sniffling, despite the lack of a cold or allergies, is a possible sign of cocaine abuse;
—long periods without sleeping. The body, quickened by the chemicals, eschews sleep for extended periods of time. Pay particular heed if your child exhibits this tendency, then "crashes" and sleeps for a similar long period;
—unexplainable change in appetite or weight. Stimulants diminish the abuser's appetite (which is why they are found in diet pills). A sudden lack of interest in food—particularly a dish which is usually the child's favorite—may portend trouble, as may dramatic weight loss. This particular sign, however, may not necessarily be one of drug or substance abuse, but of other problems, such as anorexia nervosa or bulimia. Both warrant your immediate attention;
—needle marks. Again, the abuser will probably try to hide these by wearing long-sleeved shirts, even in steamy weather.

MARIJUANA

—odor of marijuana on person and clothes. Marijuana has a strong, pungent, virtually unmistakable odor—and it's long-lasting and difficult to mask. This is a telltale sign that a person has either smoked marijuana, or it has

been smoked in their presence. Either way, it's a cause for concern on your part. The abuser may attempt to eliminate this sign by putting clothes in the wash immediately upon coming home, or by taking a quick shower before even addressing the rest of the family;
—irritated eyes. They may be bloodshot, or appear to have a dazed or expressionless appearance. The eyes, in fact, which have been referred to in poetry as windows to the soul, also provide clues to possible drug abuse. At least one NBA team has its physician walk up to each player, shake his hand and look him right in the eye before each game;
—change in level of activity. If your teen becomes quiet, melancholy, or shows general malaise, these signs may be indicative of marijuana use.

DEPRESSANTS

—acts intoxicated (slurred words, stumbling gait, etc.) but with no alcohol odor on breath;
—a pronounced, unexplainable tendency to fall asleep in unusual situations, such as at dinner, or during class. Depressants slow down the body's functions, which may prompt unwarranted sleep episodes;
—diminished interest in activities and events previously considered important. For example, a teen who had once been a voracious reader suddenly could care less about books; a youth who had been an avid jogger, but now hardly ever runs; an athlete whose entire life seemed to center around one particular sport, and

who now has lost interest in that sport; a teen who enjoyed family functions (such as picnics, parties, etc.), who now won't even consider attending such events;
—overall and chronic listlessness during the day, when energy should be high.

ALCOHOL

—alcohol odor on breath, or an attempt to mask it with extraordinary use of mints, mouthwash, etc.). Watch, too, for a tendency for a youth to refrain and shun conversations and face-to-face meetings with family members after returning home from a night out. This could be an attempt to seclude him/herself to hide the tell-tale alcohol odor;
—slurred speech. Particularly, pay attention to words with the "s" sound, which inebriated people tend to pronounce as "sh." Watch, too, for drawn-out speech and rambling, sometimes illogical, talk;
—frequent complaints of sickness or tiredness. Symptomatic of alcohol abuse are headaches and nausea. Watch for these telltale signs of hangover, and for others, such as taking aspirin or other pain reliever early in the morning; disinterest in breakfast (particularly if the teen usually eats breakfast); uncharacteristic late sleeping; and an overall grouchiness throughout the day;
—loss of interest in sports. This obviously applies to those who had already exhibited strong interest in sports, and may be a sign of the presence of some kind of a problem which should be addressed. For example, a teen

who played basketball virtually every day, and now has no desire to play at all;
— change in circle of friends. True, this is a general indication of substance abuse, but it's also particularly true with alcohol, since teens tend to drink in groups;
— lack of communication. Monosyllabic answers to questions such as "Where are you going?" "When will you be back?" "Who will you be with?" are often nothing more than a teenager's almost natural aversion to what is considered parental prying. But if the secrecy becomes furtive, and the teen displays anger at the questions, then perhaps alcohol (or another substance) is the real problem.

HALLUCINOGENS

— blank, vacant stares. Often, the abuser seems to be daydreaming, and needs to be spoken to several times before responding;
— inappropriate and extended interest in common objects. For example, examining an ash tray for a long period of time, turning it, viewing it from different angles, etc. Also, similar examination of body parts, such as a finger, hand, foot, etc.;
— anxiety caused by no apparent reason;
— PCP abusers may experience sweating episodes, salivate heavily, and have flushed skin;
— also, PCP users may have dilated pupils and may be inexplicablyhigh-strung.

OPIATES

- —raw, red nostrils (if method of ingestion is sniffing); needle marks in arms if drug is injected;
- —lethargic, drowsy behavior at inappropriate times (when person has already rested for an extended period of time);
- —inordinate and constant need for money. This is an especially telltale sign if the teen is extremely purposeful when trying to obtain the money, and won't take "no" for an answer.

INHALANTS

- —frequent runny nose and eyes;
- —odor of substance on clothes or body;
- —inappropriate drowsiness;
- —misplacement or rearrangement of household solvents, which may indicate the teen is using the substance to get high, and then returning it to its storage place.

No one knows your child better than you do, and that knowledge must be the guiding principle in evaluating any possible warning signs of substance abuse manifested by your teen. What you're watching for, mostly, is behavior that represents a somewhat dramatic change in character or previous experience.

And again, please remember: the fact that your teen exhibits some of these signs does not mark him/her as a drug abuser; rather these signs only indicate the possibility of substance abuse or of another problem—possibilities which should be explored further, as detailed in Chapter 7.

CHAPTER SIX

WHY KIDS DO DRUGS AND ALCOHOL

No simple answer exists to the perplexing question, "Why do teens take alcohol and other drugs?" Unfortunately, the answers are likely to be as varied and complex as the abusers themselves.

But several studies have been performed to help determine some of the overall causes of abuse, and their results shed some light on what motivates teens to abuse alcohol and other drugs. By understanding what some of these influences are, we, as parents and educators, are better prepared to help our teens recognize—and better handle—these circumstances which may lead them to try drugs or alcohol.

SOCIAL INFLUENCES

A 1983 study by *Weekly Reader* determined that beyond fifth grade, peers played the major role in shaping children's attitude toward alcohol and drugs; up until that point, the way drugs and alcohol were depicted on television and in the movies was determined to be the most influential factor.

After fifth grade, the influence of television and movies dipped to second.

It certainly shouldn't be surprising to find that the media plays such an influential role in shaping our children's attitudes. Think, for a minute, of how drugs and alcohol are often portrayed in those media. The hard-drinking, fast-talking successful businessman. The jive, wealthy young person who is rich, despite (or, as is often indicated, because of) recreational use of illegal drugs. The affluent Yuppies who still enjoy an occasional joint or snort of cocaine.

Too often, drugs are linked to success in the media. For proof, look no further than beer commercials on TV. Beer is always associated with good times, memorable occasions, and special people. Or, the product—beer—is hardly even mentioned in the commercial, which, instead, becomes a comedic event. Again, though, the message—however subliminal—is the same: beer and good times are synonymous.

Similarly, the message is often carried in the media that there is indeed a "pill for every ill." Advertisement after advertisement tell us how to relieve pain and discomfort. Apparently, youngsters tune into this message, and come to believe that they, in fact, should feel nothing except pleasure.

Yet, the flip side of a chemical dependency is rarely shown: the person who sits alone at home and drinks in secret; the person with slurred speech and staggering gait; the havoc a chemical dependency can wreak on a life, and on a family.

The *Weekly Reader* survey also provided an interesting insight into other reasons why teens use drugs. The findings indicated that the most compelling reason children of all ages (from fourth grade on!) used marijuana, for example, was to "fit in with others." From grades six to 12, the second major reason was "to have a good time."

THE INFLUENCE OF PARENTS

Other studies have found interesting—and strong—correlations between parental attitudes toward alcohol and other drugs and the subsequent attitudes of their children.

The 1978 RTI study discovered that students' drinking was associated with their parents' drinking behavior. Approximately 59 percent of all students with at least one parent whom they believed drank regularly were themselves moderate to heavy drinkers. Yet, only 29 percent of students who considered their parents abstainers were moderate to heavy drinkers. Eighty-five percent of high school students said they had at least one parent who drank alcoholic beverages; nine percent said both parents drank regularly.

Obviously, then, what the child sees at home—the before (and/or after) dinner cocktail, the too-many beers at the barbeque, the pushing of "one more for the road" to a visitor—has a profound impact on his/her perceptions as to the proper use of alcohol.

Influential, too, is the teen's perception of parental attitudes toward drinking. The survey showed that boys who said their parents approved of teen drinking were twice as likely to be heavy drinkers than boys who said their parents disapproved of teen drinking (35 percent to 17 percent). Similar results were found among girls.

So, the picture is coming into a somewhat less-fuzzy focus: there is no one reason that teens begin drinking or abusing other drugs, but, rather, several contributing factors. Certainly, peer pressure is rampant. Teens see their friends drinking, and perceive that these friends expect them to drink alcohol.

The image—so convincingly projected by the media—that drinking (and other forms of abuse) is part of being an adult also weighs in a teen's decision to begin abuse. Others think that abuse is just a natural part of their maturation into adulthood.

PSYCHOLOGICAL INFLUENCES

But there have been other surprising factors found, too. Those who abuse alcohol, for example, are more tolerant of, and involved in, deviant behavior, and attach less importance to religion. They also perceive the positive aspects of drinking much more heavily than the negative consequences, and they tend to have lower standards of academic achievement and expectations than those who are not problem drinkers. Also, they value their independence from parents quite highly.

Then, too, there are the internal, personal factors that may prompt a youth to try alcohol or other drugs: the feelings of adolescence, a sense of isolation, poor—or unsteady—relationships with friends; weak decision-making skills; an overstated desire for independence; and a lack of willpower.

Stress could play a precipitating factor in turning a child toward alcohol or drugs. Carol Fisher-Steinbroner, a bereavement counselor in New York State, says the unresolved death of a close friend or family member is just one of the events that may prompt a child to his first inebriating drinking episode, or his first flirtation with illegal drugs. Other events include serious illness in a family member or friend, the divorce of parents, a relocation and unanticipated academic pressures.

Also pivotal is the role of other forms of family stress, such as physical or psychological abuse. Not surprisingly, indifference—which many consider to be the opposite of love—may also be a prompting factor.

Uncertain values, goals and priorities may also be characteristic of teenagers who develop abuse problems, as are low levels of self-esteem and self acceptance.

As drinking or other abuse problems increase, there is a concurrent rise in the likelihood that the teen would experience problems with their families as a direct result of the drinking. In the 1978 RTI study, for instance, 20 percent of senior high school students—about two million teens—were estimated to have trouble with their families over drinking during the previous year.

That occurrence rate of conflict with their families over drinking increases dramatically to 74 percent among senior high school students who reported drinking while intoxicated six or more times during the previous year. Those who said they did not drive while intoxicated reported only an 18 percent incidence rate of problems with their families.

Not surprisingly, students were more likely to experience trouble with their families over driving when they took part in unchaperoned peer activities, with the highest level of drinking-related family problems occurring among senior high school students who said they often drank alone, or when they drove around at night.

WHERE TEENS DRINK

It seems apparent that certain environmental factors come into play and influence a teen to drink. This is particularly useful information, because alcohol is typically associated with initial drug experiences among youth, and the environmental factors linked with the consumption of alcoholic beverages are likely to be factors in the ingestion of other drugs. Consequently, our ability to recognize—and warn our teens about—these potential environmental pitfalls could help preclude alcohol and substance abuse by them.

Most recent research seems to indicate the earliest drinking experience comes under parental supervision, in the home, during special occasions. For example, a child may be allowed to have a minimum amount of wine or beer at Christmas, Thanksgiving, an anniversary party, or other such event. Under those circumstances—supervised by parents—teens do not tend to get drunk, and consumption of alcohol is moderate. The real trouble begins, however, when drinking occurs in unsupervised settings.

Here are the findings of the 1978 RTI survey concerning where teens do their drinking—and when:

—nearly six times as many senior high school students drink alcoholic beverages at home on special occasions as those who frequently drink alcoholic beverages during dinner at home. Some ethnic groups—the Italians, for example—often drink wine with their meals. But teens are six times more likely to be exposed to alcohol at home during a special occasion, rather than as a matter of regular dining protocol;

—45 percent of senior high school students often drank at unsupervised teenage parties, but only two million (19 percent) drank at teenage parties which were chaperoned;

—senior high school boys are more likely to drink at unsupervised teenage parties than girls. Approximately 53 percent of 12th grade boys drank at such parties, while only 45 percent of the 12th grade girls did. At supervised parties, the difference was much less distinct: only two percent more 11th and 12th grade boys than girls consumed alcoholic beverages at the parties;

—one of every four senior high school students drinks during or after a school activity (such as dances, football games, other sporting events) when adults are not present or cannot see them. Boys were more likely to drink under such circumstances than girls;

—almost one of every three high school students often drink in unsupervised teen "hangouts." Such sites could be a vacant field, a school parking lot, a park, or any other locale where adult supervision is not present. Again, boys were more likely to participate than girls;

—surprisingly, drinking in unsupervised environments among junior high school students is similar to senior high school students, only on a smaller scale. For example, both groups are twice as likely to drink at unsupervised, rather than supervised, parties;

—almost one of every four senior high school students often drink while driving or sitting around in cars at night. Senior boys (25 percent), again, were more likely to be involved than senior girls (19 percent). Another 27.8 percent of teens indicated they sometimes drank in that setting, which adds up to almost half of the students in senior high school who are drinking while sitting or driving around in cars at night. Obviously, that maximizes the risk for alcohol-related traffic accidents;

—senior high school students in small towns are almost twice as likely to drink when sitting or driving around in cars as their counterparts who attend schools in large communities;

—the odds are greater that students in suburban or medium-sized towns will drink at unsupervised parties than students in big cities or small towns;

—fewer senior high school students in big cities often drink in unsupervised settings than those in smaller communities;

—less than one of every ten senior high school students often drink alone, and that number declines to just five percent by 12th grade.

Obviously, any consumption of alcoholic beverages by minors is illegal and dangerous. But the most dangerous of the above-described situations certainly are those which involve the use of the automobile.

A number of studies conducted by RTI, the National Center for Health Statistics and the National Highway Traffic Safety Administration bear out that conclusion.

Motor vehicle accidents are the leading cause of death among our youth, aged 15–24. In 1980 alone, more than 16,500 youths died in such accidents. Males are more likely to die in such accidents than females, as 77 percent of all those youths aged 15–24 who were killed in motor vehicle accidents were males, as were 83 percent of all drivers of the same ages involved in fatal crashes.

Most auto fatalities involving 15–21 years old occurred on weekends between 11 p.m. to 3 a.m., and one of every four senior high school students was at risk, because of drinking, to be in an alcohol-related accident at least once during the previous year.

WHERE TEENS FIND THE SUBSTANCES

Unfortunately, procuring alcohol—even in states where the legal drinking age is 21—is ridiculously easy, through a variety of illegal methods. Many teens use false IDs, which are obtainable through a variety of sources, to "prove" they are of drinking age; other simply ask their older "friends" (and we use the word loosely) to purchase the liquor for them. And, sadly, there are those who will sell alcohol, without proof, to obviously underage minors, despite the absence of even a false ID card.

Drugs are most often purchased at school, usually from other students. The actual trafficking of the drug is typically controlled by an adult "pusher," but other students are the primary sales point of drugs for most teens. Using teens' peers to do their dirty work is an old trick of child exploiters. In the prostitution business, for example, a pimp will often have one of his young workers frequent bus or railroad stations, where runaways arrive, and have her "befriend" the scared youngster. Quickly, the girl is coerced into the murky world of prostitution by her new-found "friend." It's a scheme which is a proven success for virtually any type of exploitation of young people.

So, the factors which may prompt a child to try alcohol and other drugs are vast and complex; couple that with the easy availability of the substances, and you can see why so many of our children fall prey to the lure of the "high" promised by these drugs.

Yet, there are ways to short-circuit, defuse, and sometimes eliminate these factors. We'll learn about them in Chapter 8.

CHAPTER SEVEN

IF YOU SUSPECT YOUR CHILD IS ABUSING DRUGS...

It's probably one of the most frightening situations a parent must face in the life of his or her child: the possibility that the child is abusing drugs. Alcohol or marijuana. Cocaine or amphetamines. It doesn't matter what the poison is, just that the child is abusing it.

That possibility is a specter no parent wants to face, yet statistics show that millions of teens each year drink and abuse other drugs. Drug abuse and alcoholism, like so many other social ills, respect no race, status or religious boundaries. It can infect any child—yours, mine, your neighbor's.

That, of course, is the bad news. The good news is that, with help, any form of chemical dependency can be controlled, and that the earlier the abuse is detected, the easier it can be halted. So parents and educators are doing children a favor—not a disservice—by watching for signs of drug abuse.

Still, even in the face of what many would consider overwhelming evidence of drug abuse by their children—abnormal behavior, telltale odors, dramatic change in circle of friends—some parents stave off discussing the issue with their child. They refuse to believe their teen could be involved in chemical abuse. But the fact is this: the longer someone abuses a drug, the tougher it becomes for that person to eliminate it from his life. Parents who put off—in the face of near-conclusive evidence—addressing a suspected drug problem are only exacerbating the seriousness of the problem.

The manner in which you, as a parent, handle suspected drug abuse by your child is crucially important. Certainly, the child—at first—will likely be defensive to your accusations. No one wants to immediately admit (s)he's been using alcohol or other drugs. Detailed in this chapter are sample dialogues to follow as guidelines to help you if you're ever faced with the gnawing suspicion that your child is using drugs.

THE FIRST SCENARIO

This is the most obvious, and probably the easiest of all the situations to handle: you catch your teen obviously intoxicated or under the influence of drugs.

It can happen in a variety of ways: (s)he stumbles through the front door, reeking of alcohol (and, perhaps, vomit. Many first-time drinkers tend to go way beyond their limit, and the stomach mounts a vigorous—and dramatic— protest); or, the teen comes through the door, appears inebriated, but has a burnt, stale, acrid smell on his clothes—the unmistakable odor of marijuana; or, the teen appears under the influence of some drug, with no overt sensory signs, in which case the substance of abuse may have been crack, cocaine, inhalants, amphetamines, barbituates, or any other number of drugs (refer to Chapter 5 for particular signs of a wide variety of drugs).

Faced with any of those situations, what should your reaction be? At that particular moment, nothing. Confronting or accusing an inebriated, intoxicated or high teen is not a wise choice, for at least three reasons: firstly, (s)he does not have complete mental prowess at the time, and wouldn't be able to grasp the fullness of your message; secondly, what the child needs most at that minute is sleep—sleep which will allow the drug's effects to ebb; and thirdly, you, yourself, need time to calm down, collect the facts, and plan your conversation with the teen the next morning. A cool, calm, prepared parent is much more effective than one who engages in a shouting match with the teen.

The next morning, when the teen has recovered from the effects of the chemical, is time enough to begin your conversation. Then, it's important for you to establish—and your child to realize—that you are not accusing, only exploring. You are there to help, not condemn. To find out why, not to yell and rage against what the teen did. Remember, what's done is done, and it can't be erased. But you can help prevent its recurrence, and that's what your immediate goal is now.

In as normal a tone as possible, open the conversation by saying, "So, tell me about last night. You certainly weren't yourself when you walked in the door. Tell me what happened."

If the teen balks—and that might very well happen—and says, "What I do is none of your business," or "Look, nothin' happened, OK?," you must respond again in a calm manner.

"It's apparent you weren't yourself last night, and I just want to know why. We want to know why because we love you, not because we hate you or want to condemn you. We don't want your life or health to be endangered, either. And we want to talk about it now."

The teen may continue to deny (s)he used drugs or alcohol the previous night. Recite the signs you observed and be certain the teen knows it's impossible to wiggle out of this situation. "Look, when you came home last night, you smelled like you spent the night in the brewery. You hung onto the railing for dear life when you went to bed, and it's pretty obvious today—bloodshot eyes, you said you have a headache—that you've got a hangover. Let's discuss it now."

After the teen admits he used some kind of chemical the previous night, don't dwell on what or how much he ingested after those points have been verified. And try not to lose your calmness and objectivity, no matter how difficult that may seem.

Instead, seek out the why of the incident, and the with whom. Establish your teen's motives for drinking or abusing other drugs. Was it planned? Was (s)he talked into it by friends? How many others were involved? Were several drugs used and/or available? And who supplied the drugs?

At this time, you must remind your teen of the consequences of his/her actions. Gently talk about the probability that (s)he has broken the law (if underage for alcohol consumption, or if using illegal drugs), and that, more importantly, (s)he has exposed him/herself to physical harm—and possibly death.

As much as you may want to, don't turn the session into a lecture; keep it as much a discussion as possible. Show more concern than anger, more compassion than vile. Kids react better to displays of affection and care than they do to angry outbursts.

Punishment is a difficult choice that is best determined by individual parents. Some parents tend to let the first incident go, with a stern warning of what will happen with a repeat offense. That's acceptable if the teen has said—and most of his/her previous actions have verified—the fact that this was a first-time experience, and (s)he won't do it again.

To teach a lesson, other parents may deprive the teen of a valued asset, such as use of the car, for a specific amount of time. And, the traditional alternative of "grounding" may work with your child.

Does the child need counseling? Again, that depends on the teen, and the answer is tricky, at best. Most professionals say no counseling is needed if the abuse is caught and addressed by parents in the early stages of its development. The teen, especially if watched closely by family from that point on, will probably not fall back into an abuse trap.

But if the teen becomes a frequent abuser, then the answer is yes, counseling is needed. Professionals such as Gerry Shulman, the senior vice president of Addiction Recovery Center, a nationwide organization which has rehabilitated many professional athletes and media personalities, are now beginning to realize that the teen abuser differs significantly from the adult abuser, and needs different treatment methods. For example, a 30- or 45- day "reha- bilitation" period at a drug abuse treatment center is less likely to be the answer, many professionals say, for a teen as it would be for an adult. Instead, they now recommend treating the teen on an out-patient basis.

Another option is to have an outpatient evaluation of your child conducted. Such an evaluation, performed at a local rehabilitation center or by a qualified mental health care professional, will help you determine the scope of your teen's abuse problem.

THE SECOND SCENARIO

If the first scenario is the easiest, this is perhaps the most difficult: you've not really found any hard evidence your child is using drugs, but, still the signs are there: abrupt behavioral changes, shifts in attitude, perhaps some physical signs...but nothing you can really put your finger on and say with certainty, "Yes, I know (s)he's using drugs." What do you do?

Before you talk with your teen, attempt to build and document your case. Write down everything that causes your concern. If the teen has siblings, talk to them: very often, they're the first to know of any abuse problem in the family. Ask them to be honest, reminding them that confirming the presence of a substance abuse problem would not be condemning the sibling to a stiff punishment—but perhaps saving his/her life.

You may want to talk with the parents of your teen's friends. Many times, bits of fragmented evidence can be put together to form a full picture. Additionally, some of these parents may have the very same concerns you do about their children—and may welcome the chance to talk about them.

When you decide to sit down and talk with your teen, it's important that you do not manifest anger or disappointment, but only your concern. Begin the conversation in this fashion:

"I've noticed some changes in you that I'm concerned with and want to talk about. Do you have a few minutes?" Then, in a calm tone, mention all of your concerns, and conclude by asking the child if there was a reason for any of these changes.

At this point, you must remember that you, as the parent, are an authority figure, a person in a position of power relative to the teen. If you confront and accuse, the teen will react in basically the only way (s)he knows how—defensively.

Consequently, it's incumbent upon you to remain as non-confrontational as possible. Do that by controlling your tone of voice, and by making no accusations. It's much less intimidating for a child to hear the soft, loving voice of a parent ask, "Are you having some problems with drugs?" than to have a parent scream, "You're using drugs, and I know it!"

Try to determine, as in the first scenario, the extent and duration of the problem, and the drugs of abuse. Remember that though most teens start out abusing only one drug, studies show that they may move on to other drugs rather quickly.

If the teen tells you others who have been drinking/and or using drugs with him, seriously consider calling those parents to apprise them of the situation. Though some may consider the behavior of other children—quite frankly—none of your business, it really is, if you stop and think for a minute. First of all, these other teens are your child's friends, and they need help, too; secondly, as a parent, you would certainly want to be informed by another parent if your teen was involved in any dangerous practices. Few things are more dangerous to teens than drugs and alcohol.

What about treatment? Again, if the abuse has been ongoing, some kind of treatment is likely called for. Consult with local mental health professionals, school guidance counselors, or your family doctor for advice and recommendations.

One important point: if it's decided that your teen should undergo some form of treatment, then the whole family should become involved in that treatment. Dr. Shulman explains why:

"The family is an interactive system, like a mobile," he says. "Touch one part of the mobile, and the whole mobile responds. It's the human version of 'To every action, there is an equal and opposite reaction.'"

Parents of children who abuse drugs tend to feel enormous guilt, thinking they did—or didn't do—something which helped push the child into his/her current problem. You must deal with those emotions, which is another reason counseling or family therapy is an excellent option. Many families have weathered the pain of drug abuse and have emerged from the experience a stronger, more loving and more cohesive unit. Yours can, too.

EVALUATING A TREATMENT CENTER

Of course, finding the right treatment center is crucial to your teen's recovery from abuse. Shulman lists these factors to consider in evaluating any treatment center:
—accreditation. The facility should be credited by the Joint Committee on Accreditation of Hospitals, or a similar state or federal agency;
—patient population. "I would not send my child to a facility that mixes teenagers and adults in the same program," Shulman says. "The concerns are too different: an adult is talking about his relationship with his wife, while the teenager is worried about the pimple on the end of his nose. They're in two different worlds;"
—treatment specifics. "Look for a program which is specifically designed to treat chemically dependent teens," Shulman continues. Shulman says some facilities offer psychiatric programs, which are probably of little help to the teen, unless (s)he has such problems;
—the staff. "Those who like to work with kids really like to work with kids and it shows," he says. "Those who don't like to work with kids don't like to work with kids, and that shows, too." Shulman suggests observing the staff in action;
—recreational therapy. "Teens have such a high energy level, one component of a good treatment program needs to be some kind of recreational therapy, where kids could channel their energy;"
—emphasis on teen responsibility. "They should talk about actions and the consequences of those actions,"

Shulman says. "Frequently, teens have to be taught about consequences, because they haven't learned about them up until now;"

—education program. "A good treatment program should have some kind of academic evaluation, and should provide schooling so the teen doesn't fall farther behind in school," he says;

—parental involvement. "I would not send my kid to a treatment program which did not require me or my wife—or both of us—to be in treatment for some phase;"

—aftercare. Shulman says ongoing support is crucial after the teen is finished with the formal treatment.

Listed in the appendix of this book are several self-help agencies established to help teens who have drug abuse problems and their families. They are an excellent source of advice and encouragement, and may be able to locate some local support networks to help you and your family through the experience.

Remember, there's virtually no drug dependency that can't be beaten. With your help and love—and, if necessary, some professional assistance—you can help your child recover from drug abuse.

CHAPTER EIGHT

WHAT PARENTS CAN DO TO HELP PREVENT ALCOHOL AND SUBSTANCE ABUSE

Can parents take actions and steps that would undoubtedly assure their children will never abuse drugs or alcohol? The answer, of course, is no. Nothing a parent can do is a foolproof answer to the problem of drug abuse.

But parents can stack the odds heavily in their favor. They can make sure they arm themselves—and their children—with the weapons necessary to win the drug abuse fight.

The suggestions in this chapter may be somewhat surprising, because many seem to have nothing to do with alcohol or drugs at all. The reason is this: a teen's decision to abuse alcohol or drugs may be the manifestation of problems, attitudes or situations that had been festering for years during the child's development. The advice in this chapter is designed to short-circuit those problems before they occur. Much of what will be discussed involves communication with your child, building your child's self-esteem, and, in general, just creating a healthy, open family relationship. Such warm, loving, open relationships are one of the best guarantees (though not foolproof) against drug abuse—and a variety of other problems.

Other topics to be discussed include parental example, education about drugs, and the importance of establishing clear, concise ground rules about their use. Put all the information together, and you've got a sound battle plan to help your child in the war against drugs.

WHEN SHOULD I START?

When is too early to begin these techniques? When is too late? The answers are simple: it's never too early, and it's never too late. Whether your child has just been born or is 16 years old—or older—you can begin using many of these suggestions immediately. Certainly, you can't talk to a six-month-old baby about the dangers of drugs. But you can begin using the communication techniques suggested. Similarly, you may not be able to explain to a four-year-old how alcohol damages the body. But you can, by your example, demonstrate responsible use of the drug in your own life.

COMMUNICATION

If you were limited to only one choice as to how to help keep your child away from drug and alcohol abuse, this would be a wise pick. Communication shows your child you care—about him/her, the things (s)he does, friends, activities—and plays a key role in helping to ease many of the problems parents and their children face during the turbulent years of adolescence.

Yet, effective communication requires work. It involves a commitment on your part, a realization that the items you find insignificant in your child's conversation are probably of vital importance to him. These suggestions for sound communication can be utilized with any child of talking age:

—pay attention when your child is talking with you. That means turning away from the television, putting down the newspaper, or looking up from your desk, and devoting your entire concentration to your child. Make the child know (s)he's more important to you than the financial page or a football game. If it's impossible for you to give your child any time at that particular moment, just say so in a calm voice, adding, "But if you let me finish this, I can talk with you in about 10 minutes." Kids are not unreasonable, and will gladly wait for you, provided you don't constantly put them off. And you can bet your child will be back in precisely 10 minutes to resume the conversation;

—talk about the mundane things. "How," asks Gerry Shulman, senior vice president of Addiction Recovery Center, "can parents expect children to talk to them about major topics in their lives—such as drugs and sex—if they've never talked about the everyday occurrences?" He's right. Ask your child about school, play, day care, friends—anything—and listen! The foundation of true communication is this everyday, seemingly insignificant, chatter. It's irreplaceable. So, make it a point each and every day—some families do it nightly at the dinner table—to urge your child to discuss his/her day. In turn, describe your day to the family. You'll be amazed how cathartic this experience can be for the entire family, and it's one you'll look forward to;

—don't lecture. Sometimes, we carry on a monologue, not a conversation, with our children. Let the child do most of the talking, and you most of the listening;

—respect your children. That means allowing them to air their views and opinions, even if they're in conflict with yours. They have as much of a right to their points of view as do adults;

—understand your child's point of view. Remember, for example, that to a four-year-old, talking about her brand new doll may be the most important thing in the world to her, even if it bores you silly;

—don't chide a child's ideas at any age. Though they may appear far-fetched and without basis, each is the proud result of his unique thought process. Be interested in what your child has to say, even on such minor topics. Your compassion now will reap larger dividends in later years;

—remember what it was like. This applies particularly to parents of teen-age children. These teens are struggling to come to grips with their own adolescence, and it's a difficult time of life for them. Remember, when you were a 15-year-old, all your ideas probably seemed right to you, too. Acknowledge that you experienced the same conflicts yourself, and offer your support. Also, with teens, it's important to tell your child you're proud of the maturity (s)he's already achieved.

What's needed, then, for effective communication with your child are two key ingredients: compassion and understanding. Mix those well with a great gob of patience, and effective communication comes naturally.

BUILDING SELF-ESTEEM

Studies have shown that many teens who resort to alcohol or drug abuse have very low levels of self-esteem. How does low self-esteem play a role in substance abuse? Peer pressure is a major influence in such abuse, and children with low levels of self-esteem apparently lack the skills to resist this pressure. Also, deviant behavior—such as abuse, truancy, delinquency, etc.—may be an attempt on the part of the child to deal with his/her own low self-esteem.

Shulman puts a perspective on the importance of self-esteem in the abuse puzzle: "If I grow up not feeling good about myself, I take that image every place I go, and that may be worse than any kind of external stress."

Here are some ways to build your child's self-esteem:

—avoid using labels. Phrases such as "You're not as good as your sister," "How stupid can you be?" "Don't you ever learn?" and "You teenagers are all alike" are generalizations which confuse the child and dilute your relationship with him. Remember—as corny as it may sound—your child is unique, a one-of-a-kind person and should be treated as such;

—avoid far-flung putdowns. When you say something like, "You never do anything right," or "You'll never amount to anything if you keep it up," such words burn in a child's mind and hurt deeply. The best cure for anger is delay: think of what you're going to say before you say it. Remember, to a child—particularly at younger ages—you are the most important person in the world to them. If you tell them they're worthless and no good, those words may become a self-fulfilling prophecy;

—remember to praise your child. When your child's behavior pleases you, pause immediately to praise her efforts. When she does something that disturbs you, describe the specific incident and offer constructive criticism. And when reprimanding a child for an incident, make it clear it's her actions that you disapprove of—not her. Try to laud at least as often as you chide;

—don't be judgmental. If your child breaks a household rule or angers you, remember, again, that it's the action, not the person, that deserves the reprimand. Even if your child has a drug abuse problem, that doesn't make him a bad person: rather, he's a good person with a problem—a problem that can be rectified;

—imbue in your children a feeling of self-worth. Accomplish this by giving them household chores which are suitable for their age. Praise them when they complete the chores. Also, don't be afraid to tell a child—often—that (s)he is special. Because, (s)he is;

—recognize your child has some degree of responsibility. Try giving your child options, rather than orders. This builds the child's decision-making powers, and forms the foundation to help solve more difficult problems, such as saying 'no' to drugs, in later years;

—help them understand the consequences of their actions. Explain the positive and negative outcomes of your child's pondered actions. Again, this strengthens the decision-making process, and helps the child weigh all sides of an action before going ahead with it;

—don't ask your child to live up to other children's accomplishments. In other words, don't make it appear as if your love for them is tied into their academic ac-

complishments or their athletic prowess. Instead, encourage them to try as hard as they can. Then, tell them how pleased you are with their efforts;
—tell your child your love is unconditional. One of the deadliest remarks a parent can make is, "If I ever catch you drunk, I'll throw you right out of this house." Threats such as these hurt the child, and makes it appear that one misplaced act, such as drinking, is powerful enough to offset the love parents have for their offspring. Certainly, it's not. In fact, by telling your child, "I'll love you, no matter what you do," you're providing this message: "Nothing you do is enough to make us stop loving you. We're your parents, and we're here to help you, love you and give you support. Come to us with your problems, and together, we'll deal with them."

THE IMPORTANCE OF FEELINGS

Most of us have the wrong perception of feelings; we are sometimes embarrassed by them, and often try to keep them to ourselves.

The media contributes to this attitude. It's not necessary to feel pain—take a pill instead. Feeling miserable? This cold syrup will help.

As parents, we sometimes say to our sobbing children, "That's enough crying. Now, act your age."

The message is clear: don't feel bad. It makes you—and those around you—feel uncomfortable.

Unfortunately, some children grow up believing feeling bad *is* bad—and drugs and alcohol are ways to feel good for awhile. So, they turn to these substances as an escape, as a way to not feel bad.

Yet, as we all know, feeling bad is as much a part of life as feeling good. The ability to cope with bad feelings is crucial to our mental health throughout life. And so, it's important we allow our children to feel, to experience, both good and bad.

Allow your children—male or female—to cry. Avoid remarks such as, "You're too big for that," or "Boys your age shouldn't be crying." Similarly, encourage them to show their other feelings—affection, anger, disappointment—and to show them openly. Some parents, for example, don't like their boys showing overt signs of affection after a certain age, saying it isn't masculine. Yet, experts agree it's healthier for all children to display their feelings than it is to suppress them.

In any situation, then, don't be afraid to tell the child the emotions you're feeling, either, and urge him to reveal his to you, too.

Remember feelings are neither right or wrong; they simply exist. An easy way to determine if you're expressing a feeling or merely voicing an opinion is by substituting the phrase "I think" in place of "I feel." If the subject makes sense with the substitution, you're verbalizing a judgment or thought. For example, "I feel we should talk more," is an opinion, because the subject makes sense as "I think we should talk more." However, by getting to the feeling behind the opinion—"I feel sad because we don't talk enough," which doesn't make sense as "I think sad because we don't talk enough"—you're revealing your feelings, which is a major step in effective communications.

PARENTAL EXAMPLE

Your attitude toward alcohol and drugs, and the way you use them, play vital roles in shaping your child's perception of these substances. If your child sees you using pills or alcohol as an escape, then that is the way he may use them.

If, on the other hand, alcohol is used on special occasions, and in moderation, this message will get through: alcohol is for occasional use only, and is to be consumed only in limited quantities. It is not to be used as an escape mechanism, or as a substitute for confidence, or to hide or mask pain.

Similarly, with drugs, if your child sees you popping several pills a day to ease even the slightest discomfort, that is the perception he will have of drugs' use. It's better to use drugs only when necessary, of course, and to explain to your child—if he sees you taking the medicine—why you're taking it. The manner in which you treat your guests regarding alcohol also influences a child. If you won't take "no" for an answer to your offer of a drink, your child will assume it's more than just socially acceptable to drink, but that it's a social responsibility, too.

EDUCATION

Take every opportunity to inform your child about the dangers of drugs and alcohol. Remind him that drugs are wrong, illegal and can cause serious bodily harm—even death. That is a message that should begin in early childhood, and be reinforced through adolescence.

Observe closely the TV shows and movies your child watches. If a program or movie begins to glamorize drugs, point out quickly, "Yeah, but they don't show you the dark side. The alcoholic shaking for a drink. The addict willing to sell her body for her next high. The kid who dies the first time he uses cocaine. That's what they don't tell you, but that's the real story." You don't need to be heavy-handed or overbearing in this approach, just factual.

Similarly, when a news event occurs involving drugs or alcohol—the arrest of a prominent person for driving while intoxicated, or the death of a star athlete to drugs—seize that opportunity to reinforce the message, too. "See? Drugs (or alcohol) can cause nothing but pain. Maybe you get high for a few seconds, but is it worth it to die, go to jail, or to be held up to public ridicule?"

LAY CLEAR GROUND RULES, AND ENFORCE THEM

Let your child know exactly where you stand on drugs and alcohol. If you don't mind him taking a drink with your family on special occasions, fine. But let him know if that's where it ends.

Also, spell out the consequences of certain actions, emphasizing, again, that though you'll love the child no less if he's violated the ground rules, (s)he'll have to face up to the consequences. For example, on drinking and driving:

"You have a license, insurance and we let you drive the car. If you choose to drink while driving, I want you to be aware of the consequences. First of all, you could kill yourself and the people in your car. Or, you might kill some innocent person in another car, or one who's just walking down the street. You'd have to live with that the rest of your life.

"Let's say that things aren't that drastic. Let's say you just get stopped because you're swerving in traffic. Well, the penalties for driving while intoxicated in this state are pretty tough, particularly for minors. It'll cost you your license. It'll cost you your insurance. And for the rest of your life, you'll have trouble getting insurance; even when you can get it, you'll pay exorbitantly high prices for it.

"Let's go to an even lesser degree and say you did some drinking, you drove home without any problems. Should I let that go? No. If I find out you've been drinking while driving—remember, you're a minor and aren't supposed to have even one drink, let alone drive after drinking—here's what happens. We'll take you off our insurance, which effectively means you won't drive until you can afford your own insurance, or your own car, since you won't drive ours again.

"Now, I'm not saying this to be tough, just to be fair. And don't think you have some kind of magic which will protect you from having an accident after drinking, because you don't. No one has ever gotten into the car after drinking and said, 'I know I'm going to have an accident.' They all thought they could make it to their destination safely.

"You've heard all that I'm going to say on this subject. If drinking while driving is worth taking these chances, fine, go ahead and risk the consequences. But at least you know now what those consequences will be."

Remember, though, you must give them one other important option: perhaps your teen made a mistake and did some drinking, and now he has a dilemma. Does he attempt to drive home and "get away" with his drinking (which is exactly the opposite of what you want him to do)?

Instead, make this irrevocable deal with your teen: if he's been drinking and has the car, he can call you, and you'll go pick him up, no questions asked at that time. That doesn't mean there are no consequences for the drinking episodes, but those repercussions are much less than if he drove home after drinking.

In the same vein, this deal should extend to other situations, including one in which the person your teen is riding with has been drinking. Agree you'll provide a ride then, too: it's a guarantee against your child being another innocent victim of drunken driving.

GIVE THEM COPING SKILLS

How would your teen react if someone offered him some crack? Or if she was given a marijuana cigarette at a party? You probably don't know, and neither does your teen, because (s)he has never been in that particular situation.

Some teens accept the drug, simply because they don't know what to say: they don't know how to say no. Suddenly, they find themselves in an uncomfortable situation, possibly surrounded by friends who are using the drug, and they merely acquiesce to the offer.

Prepare your teen (or younger child. Remember, some kids are being offered joints in fourth grade) for such an event by play-acting the situations with them. For example, consider running through this sample dialogue with your teen, with you playing the part of his/her "best" friend.

***

Friend: "Hey, Jennifer...did you ever try marijuana?"

Jennifer: "No, and I'm not really interested, either."

Friend: "Why not? It's a great high. And it doesn't really hurt you. This stuff should be legal."

Jennifer: "Yes, it does hurt you, and again, no, I'm not interested."

Friend: "Jen, I'm your friend. Would I give you anything that's bad for you?"

Jennifer: "Obviously, you would. You're giving yourself something bad."

Friend: "I can't believe you won't try it. I guess I had you all wrong, Jen."

Jennifer: "I guess I had you all wrong, too."

***

Other sample scenarios could include what to say at a party when booze is brought in; if a stranger tries to sell a drug to your teen; or if the teen is pressured by a group of friends to try drugs.

Are all these methods foolproof? If you perform each one perfectly and devotedly, does that mean your child will never abuse drugs or alcohol?

Unfortunately, the answer to that question is, again, no. But, besides doing all that you can to prevent possible drug abuse by your child, these steps will help you to recognize drug abuse quickly, and work together to solve the problem.

CHAPTER NINE

WHAT SCHOOLS MUST DO TO HELP

Schools and parents have long been allies in helping children to grow and mature, physically, spiritually and emotionally. So, it comes as no surprise that schools—which have our children for half of their waking hours daily—must be an integral part of the effort to educate our children about alcohol and drug abuse.

Also not surprisingly, there are always some objections against such an anti-drug curriculum, sometimes voiced by parents, sometimes teachers, and sometimes school administrators.

Some parents view such a curriculum as controversial, using the convoluted logic that, "If kids learn about drugs, they'll try drugs" as their philosophical Gibraltar. Teachers, too often already overburdened, wonder where they'll find time in the day to introduce another subject. And harried administrators, already having trouble making financial ends meet, scratch their heads while trying to find money to fund the anti-drug and alcohol curriculum.

All three concerns, from the perspective of the involved parties, are certainly justified. And yet, each can be overcome with some additional thought and resourcefulness.

Parents who dislike the idea of their children being taught about drugs, for example, should be told that with such dangerous substances, it's what you *don't* know that can hurt—or kill—you. How many kids know the dangers of sniffing glue? Of "lookalike" drugs? Of marijuana, cocaine and crack? Remember, if kids don't get their information about drugs and alcohol from parents and schools, they'll get their knowledge from the streets—and that information might be wrong. Dead wrong.

Teachers and school administrators recognize the importance of drug education, and realize time—and money—must be found to provide the courses to the students. Money may be generated through a wide variety of state, county and federal grants, or through contributions from various civic and helping organizations. In some communities, parents' associations have done what was needed—cake sales, car washes, etc.—to raise the money to provide a comprehensive drug education for their children.

EDUCATION AGAINST DRUGS: THE COMPONENTS OF THE PROGRAM

How is an effective drug education program implemented? What grades should it encompass? How should it be structured?

This book is not a how-to on designing and/or implementing an effective drug education program in schools. The United States Department of Education has already done an admirable job in collecting, and making available, information on a wide variety of anti-drug curricula (see appendix for resources).

WHAT SCHOOLS MUST DO TO HELP

Instead, it is the focus of this chapter to inform you, the parents and taxpayers in your community, as to what some of the government's and experts' recommendations are for comprehensive anti-drug educational programs. We will mention and briefly explain some of the more well-known of the programs, and provide addresses for more information in the appendix of the book.

What grades should be involved in the drug education program? That depends somewhat on the curriculum selected. Several curricula have outstanding projects and lessons for kindergarteners and first graders. No, these instructions don't teach about specific drugs or their effects, but instead center on honing decision-making skills and the ability to say no.

In fact, those two components form the backbone of any sound educational program about drugs. Additionally, they help the child cope with a variety of other worrisome topics, such as sexuality.

As the child gets older, specific information is introduced about drugs, alcohol and their effects on the body. Since marijuana is being smoked, in some instances, by fourth graders, that fact alone seems to suggest the quicker we give our children hard facts about drugs' dangers, the better.

Before any program is implemented in a particular school, however, it's important a defined, comprehensive policy toward drugs and alcohol be researched and adopted.

In most school systems, the local Board of Education is the body which actually sets policy; the superintendent of schools, principals and teachers merely implement the policy.

So, it is incumbent upon each local Board of Education to adopt a responsible policy which delineates its position on drugs and alcohol within the school system.

That policy, if it is to be effective, must not only describe the board's official stance toward drug and alcohol, but also spell out proper procedures to be taken if the policy is violated.

Why is an effective policy needed? For several reasons:
—substance abuse by students—and educational personnel—can have a derogatory effect on the overall classroom experience, and seriously undermine the effectiveness of the student's education;
—with no anti-drug policies, confusion reigns. Teachers, students, administrators are paralyzed, not knowing what to do in certain situations. For example, a teacher sees a student smoking a marijuana joint: What is the protocol? Does she report to the principal? To the superintendent? To the school board? Are the student's parents informed? Are the authorities? As you can see, without a clear-cut policy, no one will know precisely what to do to rectify the situation;
—without such a policy, the wrong message is given to the student body and the teachers. In our culture, silence is often viewed as consent. The lack of a clear-cut anti-drug policy may be improperly interpreted by students as a weak attitude against drugs;
—the lack of an overall policy handicaps the entire chain of school personnel—from the superintendent to teachers to the school nurse—from identifying and getting aid for students who need help.

WHAT SCHOOLS MUST DO TO HELP 103

To help local school boards develop effective alcohol and drug policies, the Drug Enforcement Administration (DEA), which is an arm of the Department of Justice, has available a booklet entitled, "School Drug Abuse Policy Guideline." Some of its suggestions are worth repeating here:

—effective preventive education should be included as an integral part of the school curriculum;

—alcohol and drug education programs should "enable students to clarify their values, cope with their feelings, make sound decisions and develop a positive self image;"

—the curriculum should also include information on existing legislation "to help young people develop an understanding of the legal process and the legal system;"

—school personnel should "be able to identify users of psychoactive substances at an early stage and provide early intervention;"

—school authorities "should develop proactive as well as reactive measures to avoid the perpetuation" of substance abuse problems;

—a method must be developed for referring substance abusing "students and/or their families to qualified human service agencies;"

—school policies should clearly define the types of cases which will be referred to the criminal justice system, and those which will be handled in less formal ways by the school or family;

—policies should be clear regarding the "extent of confidentiality between students and counselors and teachers;"

—clear channels should be established through which the school will communicate with the family and human service and law enforcement agency.

Unless existing policy already governs such situations, the new statement must also provide release time for teachers to attend training sessions and workshops on drug abuse.

Though the school board is typically the sole authority on the approval of policy, it's wise for the board to seek out the help of many different constituencies in researching and writing the policy, including students, teachers, counselors, parents, local mental health and medical professionals, law enforcement personnel and public officials. This broad cross-section will assure a wide variety of input into the policy-making process, and help guarantee community acceptance and support of the policy.

One crucial—but often overlooked—step in creating an anti-drug policy is an effort to determine the extent of drug abuse in the school system. It's difficult to create and implement a policy toward alcohol and drugs when the actual severity of the problem hasn't yet been established.

Therefore, it's important that students—particularly in grades from fourth through twelfth—be given the opportunity to anonymously complete a substance abuse questionnaire. This could be simple or complex, but it should determine the following information:

—does the respondent drink alcohol? If so, how often, and under what circumstances?

—does the respondent take drugs? If so, which drug(s)? How often? How are they obtained?

WHAT SCHOOLS MUST DO TO HELP   105

—how many students does the respondent personally know who drink alcohol? Uses drugs?

Also effective as part of the questionnaire is a drug/alcohol awareness section, which measures the respondents' knowledge about drugs and their effects. This information helps define what the myths are about drugs among the student population.

The local police may be of aid in helping determine the drug abuse problem in the school system. Also, teachers, school nurses, custodians, administrators—all of these may have fragmented knowledge about the drug scene in the school system. It's important to bring these people together, so that a clearer picture may emerge.

Once the policy has been adopted, it must be implemented, which is the charge of the educational personnel. The support of parents and students is also important to the success of the policy, which is the reason why all these factions must be well-represented on the policy-making committee.

Perhaps the most vital part of the implementation of the policy is the actual drug education itself. This is the preventive portion of the policy, the part that will stop drug and alcohol abuse when it's easiest—before it begins.

There are a number of excellent drug-abuse curricula which have been praised by the United States Department of Education for their design and effectiveness. here's a synopsis of just two:

"Here's Looking at You, Two"—developed by the health educational staff at Educational Service District #121 in Seattle, Washington, in conjunction with the Washington State Bureau of Alcohol and Substance Abuse and the National

Institute on Alcohol Abuse and Alcoholism (NIAAA). In fact, the curriculum has been selected by NIAAA because it provides a comprehensive and coordinated program for grades K-12; is self-contained at each grade level; is sequential; is cumulative; includes a teacher training component to ensure effective classroom implementation; and has been field tested in different communities and states, and has demonstrated a positive impact through formal program evaluation.

"Here's Looking at You, Two" curriculum's basic philosophy is that the incidence of alcohol and drug abuse problems among young people will decrease if youths have a greater degree of self-esteem, if they are better able to cope with life's problems, if they have current information about alcohol and other drugs, and are more skilled at handling interpersonal relationships.

Specific educational objectives have been established for various parts of the program, including:

Information—to have an increased understanding of the physiological, psychological and social implications of alcohol and drug use and abuse; to know how to gather additional information about alcohol and drugs; to have the ability to distinguish between reliable and unreliable sources of information; and to distinguish between relevant and irrelevant information when evaluating a specific alcohol or other drug-related issue;

Analysis—to gain new skills in identifying and defining problems; gathering information, creating alternatives, and predicting the consequences associated with different choice and behaviors; identifying such factors as attitudes, values, feelings, emotions, advertising, pressures from family and peers, risk levels and habits; making appropriate analyses, and acting on the basis of a clear analysis; and evaluating the appropriateness of their actions;

Coping Skills—to be able to identify sources of stress in their lives; recognize when they are stressed and how it affects them; identify coping mechanisms to deal with stress; and determine the consequences of their coping behaviors;

Self-concept—young people are expected to increase their self-awareness by identifying what is important to them (people, places, things, values); recognizing their feelings and knowing how to express them; explain how they feel about themselves; and identifying their various roles and activities. Additionally, increases in positive self-concept are expected to lead to better skills in the identification of personal strengths and weaknesses and the development of skills in selecting and practicing changed behaviors.

The CASPAR Alcohol Education Program is a highly-successful alcohol education program which utilizes the help of teachers, students, health professionals and the public. CASPAR (Cambridge and Somerville [Mass.] Program for Alcohol Rehabilitation) has been chosen by the Department of Education for inclusion in its National Diffusion Network, a collection of programs which are recommended for school use. CASPAR is the first and, to date, only alcohol and drug abuse education program accepted by the Network for inclusion in the Department's listing.

At the core of CASPAR are 20 one-hour small group workshops for elementary and secondary teachers, guidance counselors and administrators. What may mark the program most dramatically, however, is its use of trained and paid high school peer leaders. These students encourage their teenage associates to talk openly and honestly about their own attitudes and behavior. The leaders are not trained as counselors, but as alcohol educators and group leaders. Because they are teens, the leaders are able to make greater and more candid contact with their peers, and give adult authorities feedback on the status of the alcohol situation in the community.

The philosophy of CASPAR is that in a drinking society, some teenagers need the ability to deal with problems associated with drinking. CASPAR, then, attempts to create an atmosphere in which students can explore their problems and views openly. The expectation is that teenagers who understand and evaluate their own attitudes and behaviors will feel more in control of their own experiences and be better equipped to deal with the drinking problems of friends or family members.

Early intervention is a crucial part of the CASPAR program. For example, heavy teenage drinkers are sought to be identified and helped. Additionally, CASPAR addresses itself to helping teens solve a variety of real-life situations, such as:

—refusing to ride with someone whose driving performance is impaired;
—understanding the dangers of combining alcohol with other drugs;
—confronting friends who drink and drive too much and too often;
—seeking help if alcohol is a problem for the individual or for someone is his/her family.

Unlike many other programs which seek to educate about alcohol, CASPAR seeks to help students unlearn cultural biases, and then prompt them to re-educate and re-examine their personal attitudes and values. Education about alcohol related issues, rather than alcoholism, is stressed for teenagers.

The overall goal of CASPAR is to modify youthful drinking practices through persistent learning experiences and meaningful change in the community understanding of alcohol; present a student-centered curriculum that deals with knowledge and attitudes about alcohol which can influence student behavior; and address the problems of understanding alcohol as it is integrated into society and personal value systems and philosophies.

Of course, several other programs for substance and alcohol abuse are available for school systems; these two were described briefly because they have been shown to be effective in several schools, and have been singled out for praise by various organizations of the government. Additionally, they contain the components which comprise the most successful drug and substance abuse education programs—components which belong in every such education program in every school system nationwide.

The essential point about drug and alcohol education, however, is this: it must be implemented before it can be effective. Does your child's school have a drug and alcohol abuse education program? How seriously is it conducted? Which curriculum is used? Are there any plans to modify the curriculum, or introduce a new one?

Similarly, what is the school board's policy on alcohol and substance abuse? Do teachers know how to make referrals if they suspect a student has a problem? Or is the protocol poorly spelled out?

110 TEENAGE ALCOHOLISM AND SUBSTANCE ABUSE

Realize this: you have the right to know the answers to these questions. A call to your superintendent's office will yield most of this information. If not, call a representative of the Board of Education. And if that still doesn't work, attend the next board meeting. A public portion of the meeting allows comments from the audience; use that time to question the school board about its policies, and how those policies are being implemented.

CHAPTER TEN

WHERE DO WE GO FROM HERE?

Utopia, one might argue, would be where alcohol and drugs are neither needed or wanted. Unfortunately, we live in a world that is far removed from Utopia. Our bodies occasionally need drugs to help deaden pain and speed recovery, and our psyches sometimes long for just an occasional alcoholic drink and its effects.

Does that mean the havoc caused by alcohol and drug abuse must go on? No, it does not...but before significant strides are made in the abuse battle, society's attitude toward all drugs must shift.

Recently, on a nationally-televised news program, a powerful ad agency executive defended advertisements promoting beer, saying that never once had an advertisement prompted a youngster to try beer.

Unfortunately, that's not the case. Advertising is meant to sell products, to influence attitude. Youngsters from kindergarten through fourth grade listed television and movies as the prime influences in shaping their attitudes toward alcohol; from fifth grade on, it was the second-rated influence.

That means these advertisements do have an impact. They associate beer with "kinda special" times, for example, and seem to infer that such events are difficult—if not improbable— without beer.

What must change, then, is the public's attitude toward alcohol and other drugs. They must be viewed for what they are: substances which must be used occasionally and in moderation (providing they're legal). This country tried to live without alcohol once, and couldn't. This country lives—in the face of overwhelming evidence that it's extremely dangerous to your health—with tobacco. Certainly, then, it will continue to live with alcohol and drugs, substances which, when used properly, have social and medicinal values.

What we must do is to let our children know what the consequences are of abuse. Sure, it may be "cool" to go out drinking on Friday night, but does a teen fully appreciate the possible ramifications of such a decision?

Does the typical teen see himself lying dead after snorting cocaine? Or smoking crack?

Does the everyday teen see herself arrested and in jail for possessing marijuana?

Usually not, and that's the kind of information we—parents, educators, caregivers—must give to our children. Simultaneously, we must build up the vital personality traits and skills of our children. We must work on their self-esteem, provide activities and responsibilities which will enhance their self-worth, and help them hone their decision-making and coping skills so they might be better prepared to wage battle against alcohol and drug abuse.

This book is a start. Ask your teen to read the chapter on the long- and short-term effects of drugs. Discuss the chapter with your teen. Do the same thing with other chapters in the book.

Beyond that—and, perhaps, most importantly—keep talking with your child. It's unfortunate that so many of us forget about the thrill we experienced the day each of our children were born, the feeling that nothing would ever get between us and that child. Now, the distractions of everyday life often cause us to forget about that thrill, and we watch the evening news, read the paper or balance the checkbook rather than talk with our children.

So, let's talk with our children. Let's give them the skills and information they need to "just say no." Let's help them take a stand against drugs—and for life.

Let's do it today...and every day.

TABLE I DEPRESSANTS

Drug	Trade or Street Name	Possible Effects	Possible Signs of Abuse	Dependence Physical	Dependence Psychological
Tranquilizers	Valium, Librium, Equanil	—slurred speech —staggering walk —poor judgement —slow, unsteady reflexes	—acts intoxicated, with no odor on breath —tendency to fall asleep in unusual situations —diminished interest in activities and events previously considered important —overall and chronic listlessness during day	Low to moderate	Moderate
Barbituates	Barbs, downers			Moderate to high	Moderate to high
Methaqualone	Quaalude, ludes			High	High
Alcohol	Beer, wine whiskey, etc.		—Odor on breath, or attempt to mask it —slurred speech —frequent complaints of sickness or tiredness —loss of interest in sports —change in circle of friends	High	High

TABLE II HALLUCINOGENS

Drug	Trade or Street Name	Possible Effects	Possible Signs of Abuse	Dependence Physical	Dependence Psychological
LSD	Acid	—rapid mood swings —increased body temperature, heart rate and blood pressure —dilated pupils —sweating —loss of appetite —poor perception of distance, time and limitations	—blank, vacant stares —inappropriate and extended interest in common objects	none	?
Mescaline	Button		—anxiety caused by no apparent reason	none	?
Phenocyclidine	PCP Angel Dust		—high strung	?	High

TABLE III INHALANTS

Drug	Trade or Street Name	Possible Effects	Possible Signs of Abuse	Dependence Physical	Dependence Psychological
Amyl nitrite	Poppers, snappers	—slight stimulation —nausea	—frequent runny nose and eyes —odor on clothes —inappropriate drowsiness —misplacement or rearrangement of household solvents	possible	moderate
Buityl nitrite	Rush, locker room	—coughing —sneezing		possible	moderate
Nitrous oxide	Laughing gas	—dizziness —lack of coordination —lack of appetite		possible	moderate
Chlorohydro-carbons	Cleaning fluid, aerosol paint	—headache —loss of inhibition		possible	moderate
Hydrocarbons	Propellants, gasoline, glue, paint thinner			possible	moderate

TABLE IV CANNABIS

Drug	Trade or Street Name	Possible Effects	Possible Signs of Abuse	Dependence Physical	Dependence Psychological
Marijuana	Pot, grass, reefer	—increased heart rate —relaxed inhibitions —slowed speech —euphoria —disorientation —red eyes	—odor of marijuana on clothes —irritated eyes —change in level of activity	?	moderate-high
Hashish	Hash			?	moderate-high
Hash Oil	—			?	moderate-high

TABLE V STIMULANTS

Drug	Trade or Street Name	Possible Effects	Possible Signs of Abuse	Dependence Physical	Dependence Psychological
Cocaine	Coke, crack, snow	—euphoria —increased excitement	—dilated pupils —irritability, nervousness, agression	Maybe	High
Amphetamines	Uppers, bennies, white-crosses, crystals	—dilated pupils —insomnia —increased pulse rate —decreased appetite	—"dry" mouth —constant sniffling	Maybe	High
Nicotine	Found in tobacco products		—long periods without sleeping	High	High
Caffeine	Found in coffee, tea or cola		—unexplained change in weight or appetite	Low	Low

TABLE VI NARCOTICS

Drug	Trade or Street Name	Possible Effects	Possible Signs of Abuse	Dependence Physical	Psychological
Opium	Paregoric	—restlessness —nausea —vomiting —euphoria	—raw, red nostrils (If sniffed) —neddle marks (if injected) —lethargic, drowsy behavior at in-appropriate times —inordinate and constant need for money	High	High
Morphine	Morphine, Pectoral syrup			High	High
Codeine	—			Moderate	Moderate
Heroin	Horse, smack			High	High
Methadone	Dolphine, methadose			High	High

RESOURCES—PUBLICATIONS, INDIVIDUALS

The authors acknowledge the use of the following periodicals, publications, articles and individuals as research sources for this book:

"A Growing Concern: How to Provide Services For Children from Alcoholic Families." National Institute on Alcohol Abuse and Alcoholism. Maryland: U.S. Department of Health and Human Services, 1985.

Ackerman, Robert J., "Children of Alcoholics: A Guidebook For Educators, Therapists, and Parents." Holmes Beach, Florida: Learning Publications, Inc., 1983.

Goodwin, Donald W., M.D. "The Genetics of Alcoholism: Implications for Youth." Alcohol Health and Research World, Vol. 7, No. 4, Summer 1983.

Lamar, Jacob V., Jr. "Crack: A Cheap and Deadly Cocaine Is Spreading Menace." Time: June 2, 1986.

Lowman, Cherry, Ph.D., NCALI Staff, "Alcohol Use As An Indicator of Psychoactive Drug Use Among The Nation's Senior High School Students." Facts For Planning, No. 2., NCAI, NIAAA.

Lowman, Cherry, Ph.D., NCALI Staff, "Prevalence of Alcohol Use Among U.S. Senior High School Students." Facts For Planning, No. 1, NCAI, NIAAA.

Parker, Jim. "Drugs and Alcohol: A Handbook For Young People." Arizona: D.I.N. Publications, 1985.

"Prevention Plus: Involving Schools, Parents and the Community in Alcohol and Drug Education." National institute on Alcohol Abuse and Alcoholism, U.S. Department of Health and Human Services, 1984.

Rachal J. Valley, et. al. "Alcohol Use Among Youth." Alcohol and Health Monograph, No. 1, National Clearinghouse for Alcohol Information, 1982.

"Report of the Conference on Research Needs and Opportunities for Children of Alcoholics." New York: Children of Alcoholics Foundation, Inc., April 18, 1984.

Russell, Marcia, Ph.D., et. al. "Children of Alcoholics: A Review of the Literature." New York: Children of Alcoholics Foundation, Inc., February, 1985.

Shulman, Gerald. Addiction Recovery Corporation, 411 Waverley Oaks Road, Waltham, MA 02154 (617-893-0602)

Taylor, Ronald A., et al. "Uncovering New Truths About The Country's No. 1 Menace." U. S. News & World Report, July 28, 1986.

Turanski, James J., M.D. "Reaching and Treating Youth with Alcohol Related Problems: A Comprehensive Approach." Alcohol Health and Research World, Vol. 7, No. 4, Summer 1983.

Uriarte, Rose. Addiction Recovery Corporation, 411 Waverley Oaks Road, Waltham, MA 02154 (617-893-0602)

"What Works: Schools Without Drugs, U.S. Department of Education, 555 New Jersey Avenue, NW, Washington, D.C. 20208. Individual copies available free of charge: Schools Without Drugs, Pueblo, CO 81009.

Wittenberg, Erica. "Drug Abuse: A Handbook for Parents." Arizona: D.I.N. Publications, 1983.

Woodside, Migs. "Inherited and Psycho-Social Influences." Journal of Psychiatric Treatment and Evaluation, Vol. 5, 1983.

RESOURCES—ORGANIZATIONS

The following organizations contributed information and/or advice to the writing of this book; individuals are encouraged to write the organizations for additional information.

AL-ANON Family Group Headquarters, Inc., P. O. Box 182, Madison Square Station, New York, NY 10159 (212) 683–1771.

Alcoholism Treatment Program, St. Mary's Hospital, Decatur, IL.

American Council on Alcoholism, 8501 LaSalle Road, Suite 301, Towson, MD 21204 (301) 296–5555.

Association of Halfway House Alcoholism Program of North America, Inc., 786 E. Seventh St., St. Paul, MN 55106 (612) 771– 0933.

Cattaraugus County Council on Alcoholism, Masonic Temple Building, Room 306, Olean, NY 14760, (716) 273–4303.

Children of Alcoholics Foundation, Inc., 540 Madison Avenue. New York, NY 10022, (212) 980–5860. Free literature is available on individual request.

Do It Now Foundation, P.O. Box 5115, Phoenix, AZ 85010 (602) 257–0797.

Families In Action, Suite 300, 3845 North Druid Hills Rd., Decatur, GA 30033 (404) 325–5799.

Hazelden Foundation, Box 11, Pleasant Valley Road, Center City, MN 55012 (612) 257–4010.

International Council on Alcohol and Addictions, Case Postale 140, CH–1001, Lausanne, Switzerland.

National Clearinghouse for Alcohol Information, P.O. Box 2345, Rockville, MD 20852 (301) 468–2600.

National Federation of Parents for Drug-Free Youth, 1820 Franwall Ave., Room 16, Silver Spring, MD 20902, (301) 649–7100.

National Institute on Alcohol Abuse and Alcoholism (NIAAA), Room 11–05, Parklawn Building, 5600 Fishers lane, Rockville, MD 20852.

DRUG ABUSE CURRICULA

For more information on the two drug-abuse curricula mentioned in this book, write:

"Here's Looking at You, Two"
Roberts, Fitzmahan & Associates
9131 California Avenue, SW
Seattle, WA 932–8409
(206) 932–8409

CASPAR Alcohol Education Program
226 Highland Avenue
Somerville, MA 02143
(617) 623-2080

- Reduce Medical Costs
- Improve Your Health
- Deal With Stress
- Start Your Own Business

BOOKS to Change Your Life!

- Save Money
- Become Wealthy
- Enjoy Life More
- Save Time

BUSINESS

How to make big money simply by knowing the right people!

HOW TO MAKE A FORTUNE IN FINDERS' FEES
By Jack Payne

With less than a $200 investment, you can begin a worldwide business that you can start right from your home and earn big profits. Find out how to set up a finders business, what the most profitable fields are, what to avoid, how to make a dynamic impression on your prospects, how to use business psychology to make your deal, and how to protect yourself. Includes all the business forms and information you need!

ISBN 0-8119-0346-X, *Only* **$12.95** Plus $1.50 S&H

Make big bucks in your spare time!

HOW TO EARN $25,000 A YEAR OR MORE TYPING AT HOME
By Anne Drouillard

Here are all the facts you need to become a successful home typist in no time! Discover how to build your clientele, how and when to expand, the initial financial outlay, keeping your books, rate-setting rules, getting the most from your telephone, and much more. A proven step-by-step program covering every aspect of this highly profitable opportunity.

ISBN 0-8119-0222-6, *Only* **$9.95** Plus $1.50 S&H

Do you want the best result from your "help wanted" advertising?

THE PRINCIPLES AND PRACTICES OF RECRUITMENT ADVERTISING
By Bernard S. Hodes

Executed properly, "help wanted" advertising can be the most effective method for attracting new employees. This comprehensive book, written by a leading expert in the field, shows how to get maximum results from recruitment advertising to attract applications from top-caliber candidates. It explains every possible option available to recruitment advertisers; examines the effectiveness of various media; and discusses methods. Illustrated with many sample recruitment ads.

ISBN 0-8119-0453-9, *Only* **$29.95** Plus $2.00 S&H

Computer buying made easy!

HOW TO SELECT YOUR OWN COMPUTER
By William Conslandse

A guide for beginners written by an expert with more than 25 years of experience in the computer field. This no-nonsense, easy-to-understand and concise guidebook outlines various computer applications and shows you how to determine the functions you'll want your computer to perform. It will help you to select the least expensive computer to fit your needs.

ISBN 0-8119-0596-9, *Only* **$12.95** Plus $1.50 S&H

GAMES and HOBBIES

Up-to-date information for coin collectors.

FELL'S INTERNATIONAL COIN BOOK, EIGHTH REVISED EDITION
By Charles J. Andrews

Since its first publication 30 years ago, this book has been the definitive guide to the identification and value of coins minted throughout the world. Included are the latest international prices for old and rare coins, as well as for those which are commonly in use today. No collector can afford to be without this unique and handy reference book.

ISBN 0-8119-0587, *Only* **$12.95** Plus $1.50 S&H

FELL'S UNITED STATES COIN BOOK, TENTH REVISED EDITION
By Charles J. Andrews

This newly revised and updated book is the definitive guide to the identification and value of U.S. coins. You will learn how to start a collection, how to evaluate and sell coins, and how to invest and speculate in them. Current values and price trends are provided for every U.S. coin ever minted.

ISBN 0-8119-0595-0, *Only* **$11.95** Plus $1.50 S&H

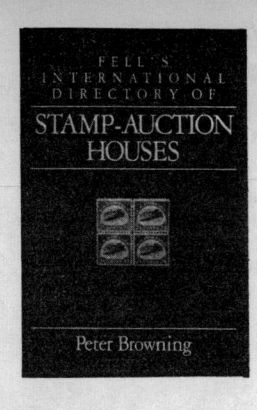

FELL'S INTERNATIONAL DIRECTORY OF STAMP-AUCTION HOUSES
By Peter Browning

"... this volume provides full up-to-date information on 350 auction houses and mail-bid firms in the United States, Canada, Europe, Asia, Australia, New Zealand and Africa." — The *New York Times*. It lists each house separately, including background material on the house, auction dates and items recently auctioned there.

ISBN 0-8119-0452-0, *Only* **$24.95** Plus $2.50 S&H

A must for every gambler!

WIN AT THE CASINOS
By Dennis R. Harrison

Now instant cash will come to you when you learn how to use the casinos to make your fortune. Contains specific guidelines for managing your bankroll, rules to help you turn your money into big winnings, and hard and fast systems that work. Beat the odds at blackjack, baccarat, roulette, craps, keno and even slot machines! This is one book you can really bet on!

ISBN 0-8119-0451-2, *Only* **$7.95** Plus $1.50 S&H

FOOD and COOKING

How to turn any dinner into an adventure in romance!

COOKING FOR THE ONE YOU LOVE
By Lucy Cole

Noted food consultant and world traveler Lucy Cole has developed this collection of easy-to-follow, elegant dinner menus for two from 24 countries spanning the Mediterranean, Europe, the Far East and the Tropics. Travel the realms of international gourmet dining in the intimacy of your own home.

ISBN 0-8119-0448-2, *Only* **$16.95** Plus $1.50 S&H

The best written cookbook ever!

THE IOWA WRITERS' WORKSHOP COOKBOOK
Edited by Connie Brothers

Recipes from more than 100 renowned fiction writers and poets, including John Irving, Anne Tyler, Raymond Carver and Galway Kinnell. All contributors are, or have been, associated with the University of Iowa Writers' Workshop. Served with witty anecdotes, poems, and caricatures, these recipes range from the outrageous to the fun-filled and the succulent.

ISBN 0-8119-0690-6, *Only* **$9.95** Plus $1.50 S&H

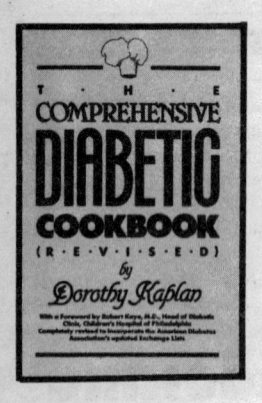

How to cook for the diabetic.

THE COMPREHENSIVE DIABETIC COOKBOOK, REVISED
By Dorothy J. Kaplan

This highly acclaimed cookbook offers easy-to-follow, step-by-step solutions to meal planning for the diabetic. "Kaplan's sensible... manual will guide the home cook in preparing meals for diabetics and weight watchers without alienating more fortunate family members." — *Publisher's Weekly*.

ISBN 0-8119-0490-3, *Only* **$8.95** Plus $1.50 S&H

COOKING FOR TWO WHEN MINUTES MATTER
By Lucy Cole

This book provides a splendid variety of exciting, creative, and delicious menus especially tailored for two people. Epicurean arrangements from all over the world are included, yet each calls for easily purchased ingredients and takes no more than an hour to prepare. For the cook with everything but time!

ISBN 0-8119-0644-2, *Only* **$9.95** Plus $1.50 S&H

Eat at the best restaurants in the U.S. without leaving home!

AMERICAN RECIPE COLLECTION
Edited by Sandy Lesberg

Now, for the first time, the Master Chef's Institute, the prestigious organization of the most celebrated chefs and restaurants in the world, presents the best of American cuisine. Under the supervision of noted American food critic Sandy Lesburg and in collaboration with Diners Club International and Carte Blanche, the institute has compiled this exciting two-volume cookbook full of delicious, mouth-watering recipes from 600 of the finest restaurants in the United States.

ISBN 0-8119-0707-4 and 0-8119-0710-4, *Only* **$9.95** Each Plus $1.50 S&H

SPORTS

Learn tennis from a pro!

KEN ROSEWALL ON TENNIS
By Ken Rosewall

Written by professional tennis star Ken Rosewall, this book outlines everything you need to know to play like a pro. It provides detailed information on grips, footwork, forehand, backhand, serve, volley, half-volley, smash, lob and drop shots. Fully illustrated with step-by-step photographic instructions.

ISBN 0-88391-080-2, *Only* **$14.95** Plus $1.50 S&H

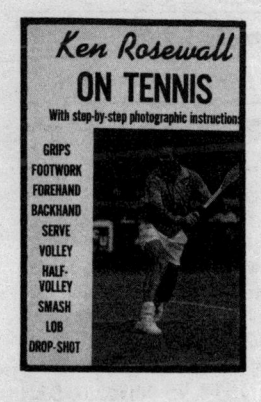

A complete diving handbook.

FELL'S OFFICIAL GUIDE TO DIVING
By Harry Froboess

A comprehensive guide and valuable instruction book for everyone interested in the art of diving; the beginner, the competitor, and the instructor. It covers plain, high, fancy, platform, comedy and acrobatic diving. A prospective champion may profit from this book, but it is designed mainly for the great masses of aquatic-minded youths of both sexes who seek enlightenment, constructive guidance and information on how the facinating sport of fancy diving may benefit them in skillful, healthy exercise.

LC Card No. 65-15502, *Only* **$2.45** Plus $1.50 S&H

How to enjoy the freedom of motorcycling safely.

FELL'S BEGINNER'S GUIDE TO MOTORCYCLING
By Bill Kayping

Bill Kayping got his first motorcycle as a gift back in 1940. He still enjoy's life by riding motorcycles and helping others to learn this exciting and rewarding sport. This book teaches safety tips, driving techniques and basic maintenance.

ISBN 0-8839-051-9, *Only* **$3.95** Plus $1.50 S&H

HEALTH and FITNESS

Tired of fad diets and broken promises? Here's what you've been looking for!

THE ROCHESTER DIET
By Paul Chereakasky, M.D.

Now you can lose weight via a custom-made diet. This innovative diet consists of a three-fold program of diet, exercise and behavior modification. For variety and flexibility, you're allowed to choose your own menus, from food items listed in the book, that are nutritious and well-balanced. This easy-to-understand manual explains everything you need to know about obesity and diet to help you become slimmer, and lead a healthier, happier life!

ISBN 0-8119-0488-1, *Only* **$14.95** Plus $2.00 S&H

Chew! Smile! You can with the miracle of dental implants.

WITHOUT DENTURES
By Leonard I. Linkow, D.D.S.

Dr. Linkow, a pioneer in the technique of dental implants, explains this remarkable process which eliminates the embarrassment and suffering associated with removable dentures, bridges and loose or missing teeth, and discusses the cosmetic, anatomic, economic and psychological whys and advantages of this revolutionary method over dentures.

ISBN 0-8119-0713-9, *Only* **$9.95** Plus $1.50 S&H

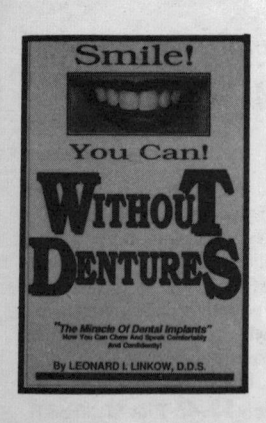

Everything you need to know to limit your intake of cholesterol, sodium and calories, yet still eat well!

HEART WATCHERS' COMPLETE DIET AND MENU PLANNER
By Sylvan R. Lewis, M.D.

Cardiovascular disease is currently America's number one health problem, yet there are definite preventative measures that can decrease the threat of this killing disease. Dr. Lewis identifies the eight major risk factors believed to contribute to cardiovascular disease and discusses methods of controlling these factors. This helpful guidebook includes a 30-day menu plan; an easy shopping guide; more than 100 low-cholesterol, low-sodium, low-calorie recipes; and cholesterol, sodium and calorie listings for more than 1,000 foods.

ISBN 0-8119-0719-8, *Only* **$6.95** Plus $1.50 S&H

At last, relief from Premenstrual Syndrome!

PREMENSTRUAL SYNDROME: A SELF-HELP GUIDE
By Wendy Van Biert Rappoport

This is an indispensable guide and sourcebook for the 40% of all American women who suffer the monthly collection of symptoms known as Premenstrual Syndrom (PMS). Readers learn what it is, how to conquer it and where to go for help. It's many charts, photos and forms encourage the reader to take an active role in her own recovery.

ISBN 0-936320-19-2, *Only* **$4.95** Plus $1.50 S&H

Hope and encouragement for those faced with breast cancer.

NOTHING'S CHANGED: DIARY OF A MASTECTOMY
By Dorothy Abbott

This joyous book is an inspiring diary revolving around Mrs. Abbott's mastectomy, beginning with the day she first felt the lump in her breast and ending with the joyous second anniversary of her operation. In this warm, inspiring, and sometimes even funny book, Mrs. Abbott describes her day-to-day reactions to her mastectomy and its influences on her life.

ISBN 0-8119-0423-7, *Only* **$11.95** Plus $1.50 S&H

Have natural childbirth after caesarean!

YOU DON'T NEED TO HAVE A REPEAT CAESAREAN
By Nicki Royall

This book, written by a mother who had a vaginal delivery after a caesarean one, includes comprehensive information and actual delivery reports of true birth experiences, and outlines ways to avoid initial caesareans, how to prepare for a vaginal birth after a caesarean, and how to get in touch with the right organizations to help you. Free yourself from unnecessary surgery and make your birth experience one you'll remember forever.

ISBN 0-8119-0487-3, *Only* **$14.95** Plus $2.00 S&H

Save your child from the pain of endless ear infections!

EAR INFECTIONS IN YOUR CHILD: THE COMPREHENSIVE PARENTAL GUIDE TO CAUSES AND TREATMENTS
By Kenneth Grundfast, M.D., and Cynthia J. Carney

This helpful guide describes exactly what an ear infection is, explains in detail the current courses of action prescribed by physicians, and examines the appropriateness of antibiotics and surgery. Written clearly and concisely by an ear, nose and throat practitioner and a writer whose child suffered through the agony of persistent ear infections.

ISBN 0-936320-22-2, *Only* **$14.95** Plus $2.00 S&H

Get rid of unwanted fat through the miracle of liposuction!

SCULPTURING YOUR BODY: DIET, EXERCISE AND LIPO (FAT) SUCTION
By John A. McCurdy, Jr., M.D., F.A.C.S.

This new book thoroughly discusses the revolutionary new French technique of body sculpturing by liposuction, a lifelong program of controlling fat based on an understanding of the basic principles of fat metabolism, proper nutrition and exercise. Written for the layman by Dr. John McCurdy, a plastic surgeon with a private practice in Hawaii.

ISBN 0-8119-0716-3, *Only* **$12.95** Plus $1.50 S&H

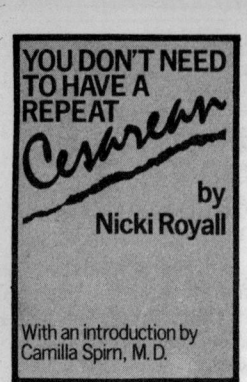

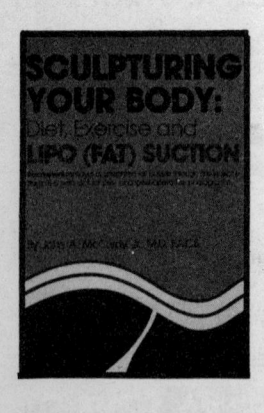

Everything you always wanted to know about eyes and more!

THE COMPLETE GUIDE TO EYECARE, EYEGLASSES AND CONTACT LENSES, REVISED EDITION

By Walter J. Zinn, O.D., F.A.A.O. and Herbert Solomon, O.D.

Here is up-to-date information on all the remarkable advances in eye care. It includes detailed descriptions of: how the eye works; how to chose an optometrist; what to expect from an eye exam; causes of specific symptoms; recognizing potential problems; eye care for children and senior citizens; and a discussion of how athletes' can protect against eye damage, light and glare.

ISBN 0-8119-0642-6, *Only* **$9.95** Plus $1.50 S&H

An indispensable guide for arthritis sufferers!

HOW TO STOP THE PAIN OF ARTHRITIS

By Professor Henry B. Rothblatt, J.D., L.L.M., Donna Pinorsky and Michael Brodsky

Based upon the theories of arthritis specialist Dr. Robert Liefmann, this book outlines his amazingly effective program for the treatment of arthritic diseases. Thousands of patients provide living testimony to the healing power of his Holistic Balanced Treatment, which, without painful surgery or numbing drugs, actually helps the body to rebuild its own healthy tissue. A simple diet and exercise program supplements the Holistic Balanced medication to strengthen those parts of the body which have been injured by arthritis.

ISBN 0-936320-23-0, *Only* **$4.95** Plus $1.50 S&H

Finally, a comprehensive guidebook for herpes victims.

HERPES: PREVENTION AND TREATMENT

By Donald A. Kullman, M.D., and Joel Klass, M.D.

This is a comprehensive and authoritative guide to the prevention, recognition and lesions, symptoms and treatment of herpes virus infections. Hundreds of the most commonly asked questions are expertly answered by practicing physicians. It includes information on all of the latest discoveries and how they can be made to work for you.

ISBN 0-936320-14-1, *Only* **$3.95** Plus $1.50 S&H

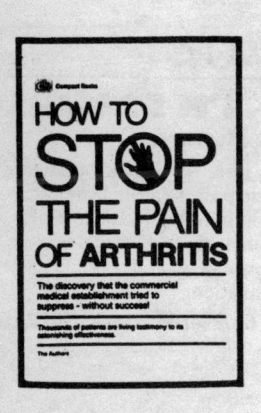

SELF-HELP

Is your marriage on the rocks?

Your divorce can be even worse —

unless you know all the dirty tricks!

DIVORCE DIRTY TRICKS
By R.H. Morrison

At last, a manual of guerrilla warfare for the man or woman who wants protection against unfair laws, an overly demanding spouse and unscrupulous, greedy lawyers. This book shows you how to get (or keep) what's yours by being a cunning, hard-bargaining, no-nonsense, down and dirty fighter. It's a complete education in divorce strategy and tactics.

ISBN 0-937484-03-2, *Only* **$14.95** Plus $1.50 S&H

Learn how to fight back!

HANDS OFF . . . I'M SPECIAL
By Dan Lena and Marie Howard

This husband and wife writing team focuses on developing the self-esteem, assertiveness and positive attitude necessary to defend oneself against assault in today's violent society. Major topics include: the different types of sexual assault, how to develop assertiveness, date rape, and how to recognize a potentially dangerous situation.

ISBN 0-936320-30-3, *Only* **$6.95** Plus $1.50 S&H

Help fight the scourge of alcohol

and chemical abuse by teens.

TEENAGE ALCOHOLISM AND SUBSTANCE ABUSE: CAUSES, CONSEQUENCES AND CURES
By Carmella and John Bartimole

This book dissects the problem of alcoholism and substance abuse among teenagers, probes its causes, and identifies the warning signs that indicate a chemical dependence. Helpful information is also included on: where and how to get help; situations which may instigate abuse; and ways to prevent children from developing a chemical dependency.

ISBN 0-936320-18-4, *Only* **$6.95** Plus $1.50 S&H

If you want a college education for your children, you can't afford not to read this!

FELL'S GUIDE TO COLLEGE MONEY FOR THE ASKING IN FLORIDA, 1987-1988
By Charles T. Mangrum II, Steven S. Strichart and Peggy Loewy-Wellisch

This comprehensive guide gives detailed information about how to apply for the large number of grants, scholarships and loans available at two-year colleges, four-year colleges and universities. It also includes information about federal financial assistance available at colleges and universities throughout the United States.

ISBN 0-8119-0706-6, *Only* **$13.95** Plus $2.00 S&H

What every parent should know to protect their child.

PREVENTING MISSING CHILDREN: A PARENTAL GUIDE TO CHILD SECURITY
By Carmella and John Bartimole

Based on a comprehensive study of who abducts and molests children and what their motivations and tactics are, this book outlines a step-by-step course parents can take to protect their children. This timely, authoritative guide includes eye-opening interviews with six convicted child molesters and one child rapist, as well as invaluable listing of character clues to help spot potential molesters.

ISBN 0-936320-21-0, *Only* **$4.95** Plus $1.50 S&H

Problem solving through hypnosis.

HOW TO HYPNOTIZE YOURSELF AND OTHERS
By Rachael Copelan

Do you want to quit smoking, or maybe lose those extra pounds? Is there a pain you wish you could get rid of for good? This exciting book will show you how to relax and take care of these problems and more through self-hypnosis. It will enable you to tap your brain's resources for positive, controlled energy, and soon unwanted behavior will be gone and a new self-image will emerge. Contains dozens of actual case histories and techniques for solving more than 350 problems with hypnosis.

ISBN 0-8119-0418-0, *Only* **$10.95** Plus $1.50 S&H

INSPIRATION

The secret of this success!

THE STORY OF PAUL J. MEYER: THE MILLION-DOLLAR PERSONAL SUCCESS PLAN
By Gladys W. Hudson and Lois Smith Strain

How does one progress from a life insurance salesman to become the founder and chairman of the board of the world's largest manufacturer in the field of personal development? The answer lies in the experience of Paul J. Meyer, chairman of the board of SMI International, Inc., a company he founded in 1960 that now produces materials in 11 languages and markets them in more than 60 countries. Meyer's quest for achieving his own goals led him through the progressive realization of expanded goals — a process that he believes to be possible for everyone.

ISBN 0-8119-0720-1, *Only* **$14.95** Plus $1.75 S&H

This woman's victory in life will touch your heart!

A STAR TO STEER BY
By Patricia Sampson

Patricia Simpson is a very special woman. Mother. Poet. Philosopher. Dreamer. Achiever. Survivor. Her philosophy of courage and commitment, outlined in this book, proves itself in her life and the lives of five of our country's most honored citizens. You will want to keep this book by your side. It will embrace you and inspire you and comfort you whenever you need a friend.

ISBN 0-8119-0301-X, *Only* **$9.95** Plus $1.50 S&H

The complete works of Og Mandino!

THE GREATEST SALESMAN IN THE WORLD
By Og Mandino

This first in a series of popular books by Og Mandino recounts the legend of Hafied, a camel boy who lived a thousand years ago and came into the possession of ten ancient scrolls which contain the wisdom necessary for the boy to achieve all his ambitions. The miraculous success that they helped him to achieve, they can help you achieve too!

ISBN 0-8119-0067-3, *Only* **$10.95** Plus $1.50 S&H

THE GREATEST SECRET IN THE WORLD
By Og Mandino

This second in a series of books by Og Mandino reproduces the Ten Great Scrolls of Success from his first book, *The Greatest Salesman in the World*, and offers a no-holds-barred explanation of each scroll. The inspiration and wisdom contained in this volume will bolster your courage through life's darkest hours.

ISBN 0-8119-0212-9, *Only* **$10.95** Plus $1.50 S&H

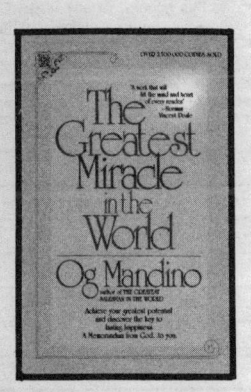

THE GREATEST MIRACLE IN THE WORLD
By Og Mandino

Here is a book that will shake you to the core. It dares you to read it and to understand its powerful message. In an almost miraculous way, it will help you to open the gates to happiness and success that can eventually change your life.

ISBN 0-8119-0255-2, *Only* **$10.95** Plus $1.50 S&H

THE GREATEST GIFT IN THE WORLD
By Og Mandino

This beautiflly illustrated version of Og Mandino's popular and inspirational book, *The Greatest Salesman in the World*. Printed in large, easy-to-read type with more than 30 beautiful illustrations.

ISBN 0-8119-0274-9, *Only* **$10.95** Plus $1.50 S&H

Books To Change Your Life

2131 Hollywood Boulevard, Suite 204, Hollywood, Florida 33020
Telephone: (305) 925-5242.

1. ORDERED BY:

Name _____

Address _____

City _____ State _____ Zip _____

Daytime Phone Number _____

(Speeds order should we have questions)

OUR GUARANTEE

1. We *guarantee* your satisfaction.
If for any reason you aren't happy with your purchase, send it back for a 100% refund.

2. We *guarantee* the quality of everything we sell.
If you think something doesn't measure up to your description of it, send it back for a 100% refund.

3. We *guarantee* unconditionally for two full months.
We don't just let you have a quick look before you have to decide whether or not you really want what you've bought. At any time within 60 days, return it undamaged for a 100% refund.

Qty.	Item #	Description of Item	Price Each	S&H each	Total S&H	Total Price

*ABOUT SHIPPING and HANDLING (S&H) CHARGES

If the total shipping and handling charges exceed $5 for entire shipping and handling, we'll absorb the additional expense. Sorry — no C.O.D. or open account orders accepted. **See below for credit card orders.** Do not send cash.

Florida Residents Add 5% Sales Tax _____
Total S&H (maximum $5) _____
Total of Order $ _____

My Method Of Payment Is: ☐ Visa   ☐ MasterCard   ☐ American Express
☐ Diners Club   ☐ Other   ☐ Check   ☐ Money Order

We cannot accept credit card orders for less than $20. If your order totals less than $20, please mail a check or money order.

(Credit Card Number)

Card Expires _____ Signature _____